Paper BUGS!

Easy-to-make Origami
Grasshoppers, Cockroaches,
Spiders, Bees, Flies, and More!

Carmel D. Morris

Paper Bugs!

Copyright 2011, 2016, Big One Productions
First published by Harper Collins 1991 as *Fold Your Own Creepy Crawlies*.
Reprinted 1992, 1993, English editions, plus Español, Deutsch,
Français, Italiano, Nederlands, Português editions.
This edition published by Big One Productions, 2015
ISBN: 9781475012606
Cover design and photography: C Morris
Typeset in Mister Earl LT, Franklin Gothic, and Palatino Linotype
This edition printed in the United States of America
10 9 8 7 6 5 4 3 2
The right of Carmel D. Morris to be identified as the author has been asserted
in accordance with the Copyright, Designs and Patents Act, 1988
Apart from any fair dealing for the purpose of review, private study, research
or criticism, as permitted under the Copyright Act, no part may be
reproduced by any process, including digital and apps, without written
permission.

Contents

Preface 5
Introduction 7
Folding Techniques 9
Base Folds 11
Caterpillar 21
Scorpion 24
Dragonfly 31
Snail 40
Cockroach 45
Butterfly 54
Bee 62
Fly 69
Spider 76
Grasshopper 84

Paper Bugs!

Preface

From the author of *The Best Advanced Paper Aircraft* and *Paper Boats!* this fun bug-building book will have all the family folding.

If you like origami but find it difficult to make complicated models, this book covers all bases; from simple to moderately complex, the author is happy to use the occasional scissor snip to meet the skill-level of those not familiar with origami. Origami modelling has a limited number of points in the malleability of paper for various outcomes; animals, geometric bodies, cars, boats, houses, and so on. To get more points, that is, more legs and antennae for six-legged bugs, let alone eight, sometimes a little snipping is done, but the outcome is worth it. While there are other books that have more complicated folds, we do not want to discourage the young budding bug-builders, but foster an appreciation of the importance of the insect world through paper folding.

Important note to entomologists

No six-legged or eight-legged creatures were harmed during the making of this book. Folded models may be useful in general educational scenarios where anatomy is to be explained. We need to protect our environment and that not only means protecting mammals and amphibians, invertebrates also require respect. Where you can substitute a paper model for explanation, you will be making a live critter real happy.

Important note to folders

Some insects in this book are more complicated than others. It is very important to practice all the basic steps described at the beginning of this book, before starting on the models themselves.

Measurements are provided in centimeters. By following the symbols, folding guides and instructions in this book, your critters are sure to be more realistic when finished.

Finally, you should be able to make convincing little critters without tearing your hair out, unlike some other books out there. So grab a sheet of colored square paper and start folding. You could also use photocopy paper, fold a diagonal and snip off the unwanted end to make a square, as shown below...

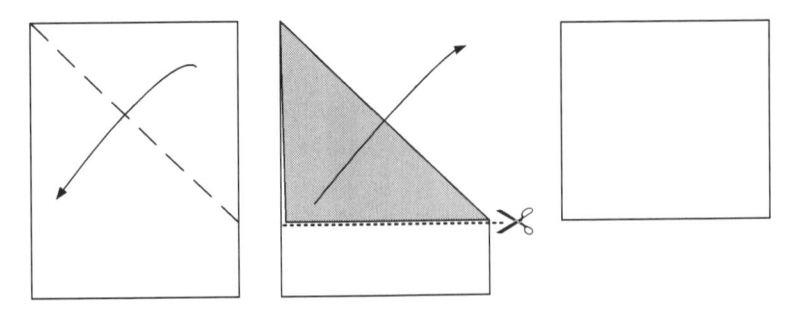

You'll amaze your buddies with your newfound origami skills. And make sure you make lots of these critters for your summer vacation or Halloween, or whatever the occasion is, for some neat creepy crawly decorations.

Happy folding!

Dwight Edwards

Introduction

Welcome to the tiny world of paper insects! Or possibly not so tiny: the beauty of using paper is that you can choose to make your bugs any size you wish – ideal for Halloween.

Insects have always fascinated me. I am amazed that something so small could be constructed so perfectly. Most people think of insects as pests, but this is only true when they appear in great numbers. Insects are in fact an important part of the environment and the food chain.

Insects are also fun. If you don't have a garden and are unable find the real variety, paper ones can be the next best thing. You could make a butterfly mobile using colored paper or prepare a school project using paper critters on real foliage. The possibilities are endless.

If you find you are having trouble making the bugs, go through the steps carefully and unfold if necessary. As for software design, in origami this is aptly called 'debugging'.

Some models require the careful use of scissors to create legs or wings. It's a good idea to have a parent or teacher handy when you need to use scissors. You might find making paper critters difficult at first, but when you build up your folding skills and eventually invent your own eight-legged, eight-eyed, double-fanged spider complete with a web that has trapped two paper flies; you'll know that it was worth it!

Types of paper to use

Most of the models in this book are made from square paper, but the size is up to you. I suggest you begin with larger sheets of paper. Any Letter or A4 sheet made into a square is ideal. When you have perfected your folding, try using smaller pieces to get that realistic life-size effect, or experiment with colored and patterned paper. Multi-colored wrapping paper would be ideal for the butterfly. You could also use textured paper to give a more creepy feeling when you sit your bug on your friend's arm. :)

Remember to protect the environment and first only practice with old paper found around the house, such as junk mail.

Folding Techniques

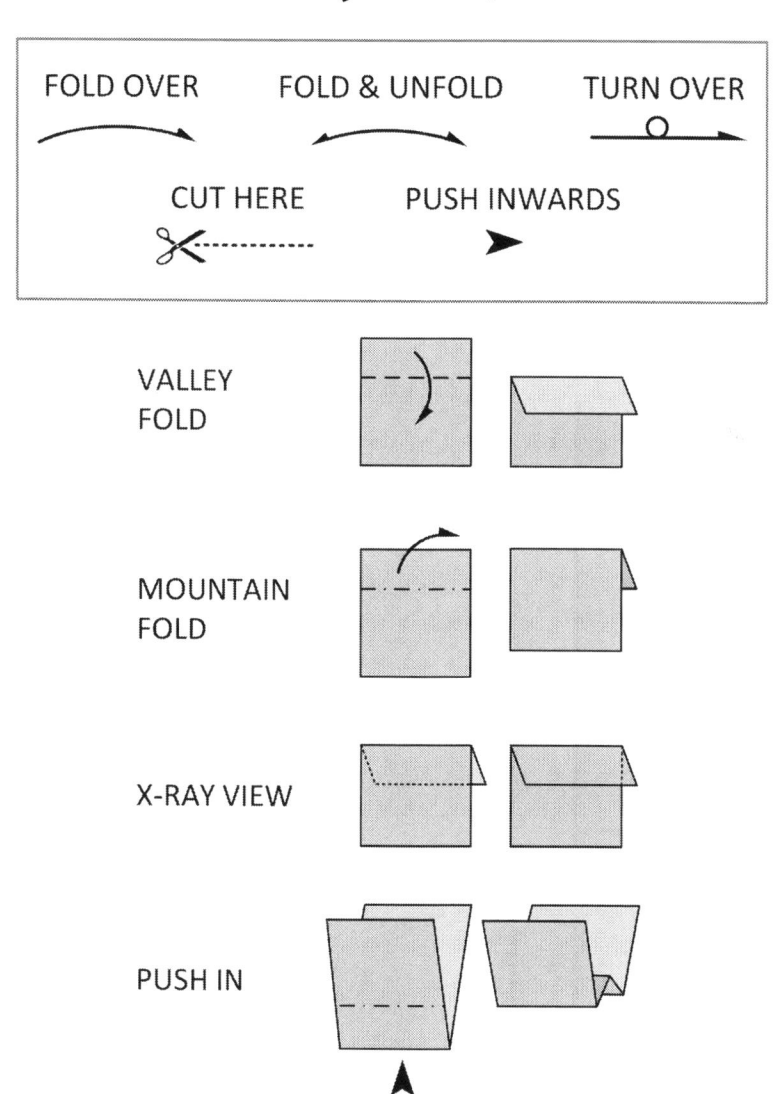

FOLD OVER

FOLD & UNFOLD

TURN OVER

CUT HERE

PUSH INWARDS

VALLEY FOLD

MOUNTAIN FOLD

X-RAY VIEW

PUSH IN

REVERSE FOLD

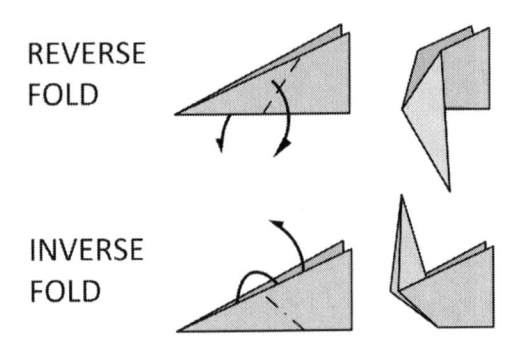

INVERSE FOLD

Rabbit Ear Fold

Make a diagonal crease-fold, and then two intersecting crease-folds. Bring in the sides and pinch together to form a point, and then flatten the point.

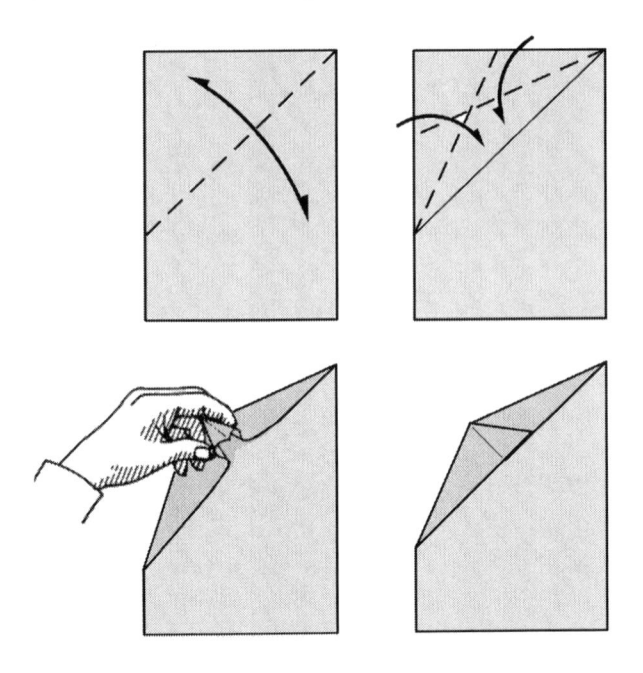

Base Folds

Two base folds are required for making most of the bugs in this book, the Preliminary Base and the Bird Base (called the Bird Base because many origami birds are made using this basic fold, including the famous crane). Familiarize yourself with these before you start folding the more complicated critters in this book.

Preliminary Base

Step 1

Begin with a square piece of paper and fold it in half from corner to corner and unfold.

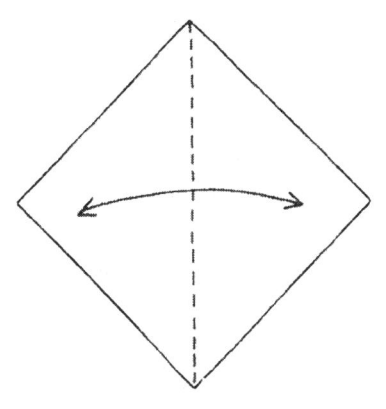

Step 2

Fold in half again as shown, and unfold.

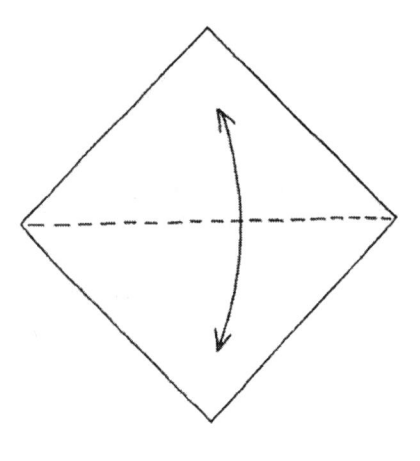

Step 3

Turn the paper over.

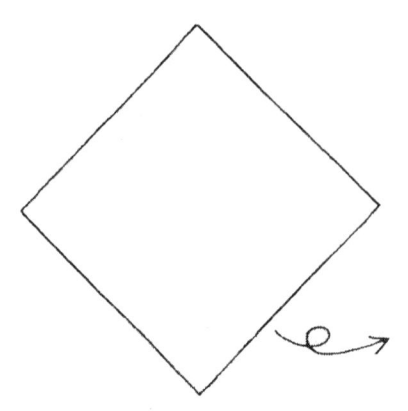

Step 4

The valley folds are now mountain folds; although not very well represented here, the folds will be pitched slightly from each diagonal axis to a center point.

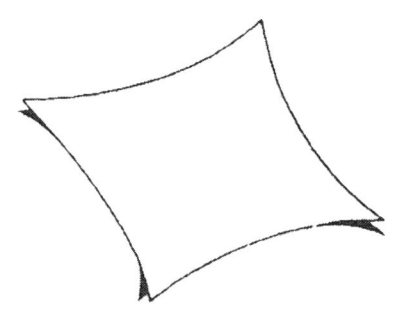

Step 5

Fold and unfold to establish (valley-fold) crease.

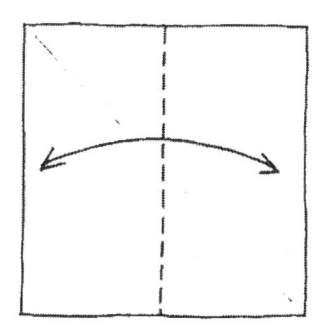

Step 6

Fold the model in half along opposite axis to the one you just folded.

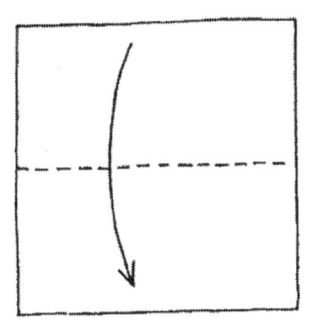

Step 7

Holding the sides together, push the corners into the center.

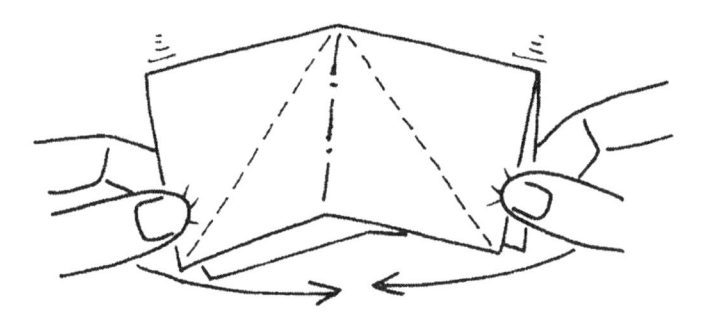

Step 8

Flatten the model.

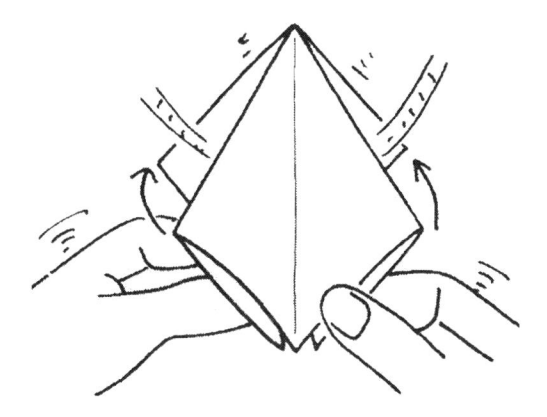

Step 9 – Finished Base Fold

This is the completed preliminary base. Many models (such as origami frogs) are made from this base fold. From here you can also make the Bird Base (as indicated by the first step in the Bird Base).

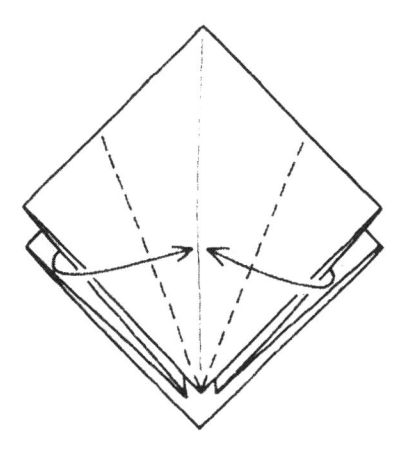

Bird Base

Step 1

Commence with the Preliminary Base (shown in the preceding instructions). Fold the front flaps into the centre crease.

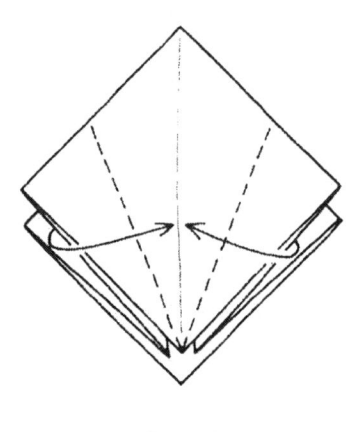

Step 2

Fold the top corner in.

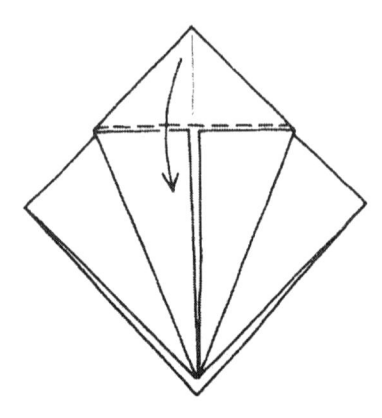

Step 3

Unfold both side flaps.

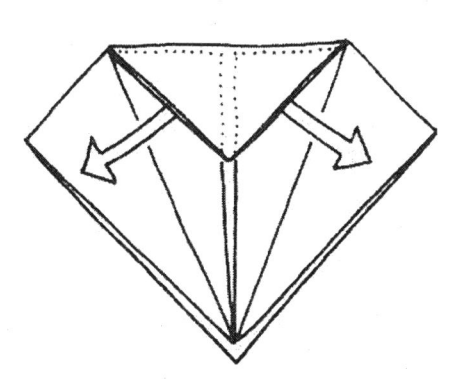

Step 4

Your model now looks like this.

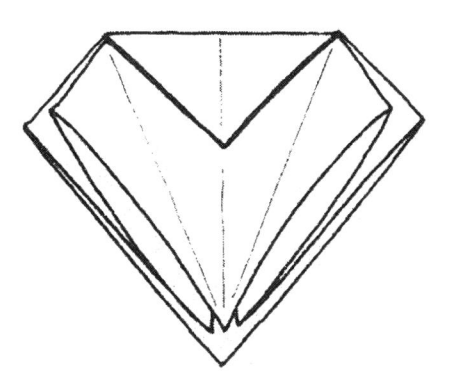

Step 5

With one hand hold all but the top flap and with the other hand fold back the top flap.

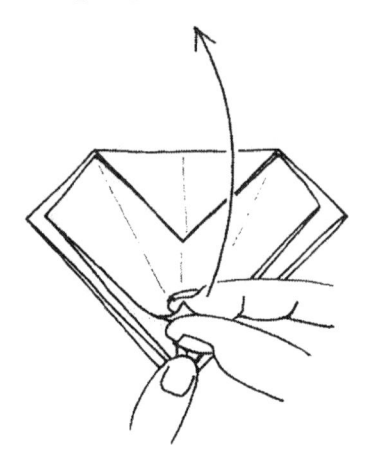

Steps 6 and 7

The sides will automatically start to fold in; press them firmly in place and then turn the model over.

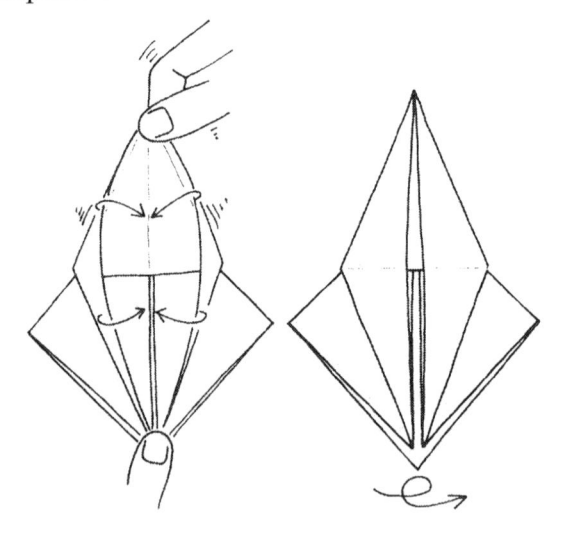

Step 8

Repeat for the other side.

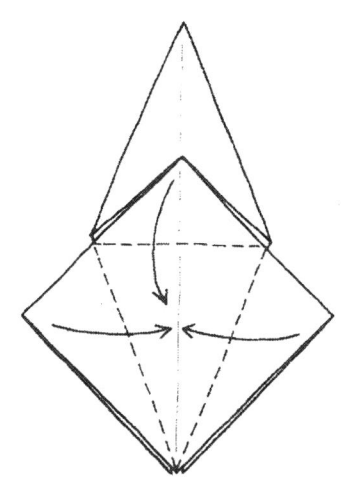

Steps 9 and 10

Fold the top flap up and press the sides into the center.

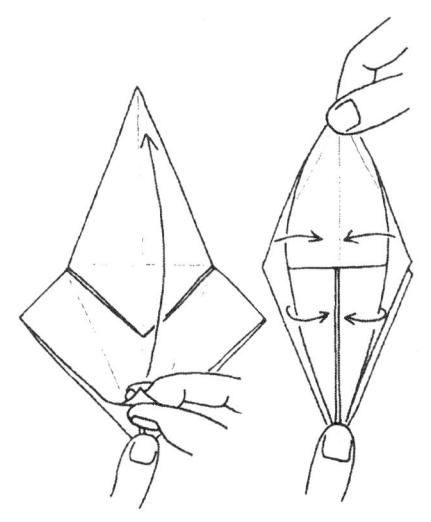

Step 12 – The completed Bird Base

From here you are ready to make the many insects in this book that use the Bird Base.

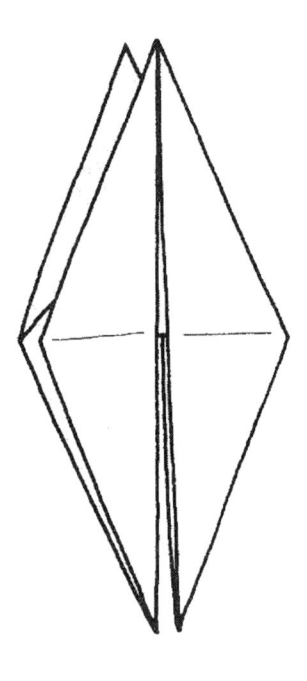

Caterpillar

This is a nice, simple bug to start with. A caterpillar is the larva form of a butterfly or moth. Caterpillars have a ferocious appetite for leaves and sap. They come in all kinds of colors and textures; often fuzzy, sometimes poisonous. Unlike the other models in this book, you don't need to start with a square piece of paper.

Step 1

Begin with a strip of paper 297 x 40 mm long (taken from a sheet of A4 paper). Crease the paper in half lengthwise, and then make stair-step folds in the six positions shown. The two end segments should be slightly longer.

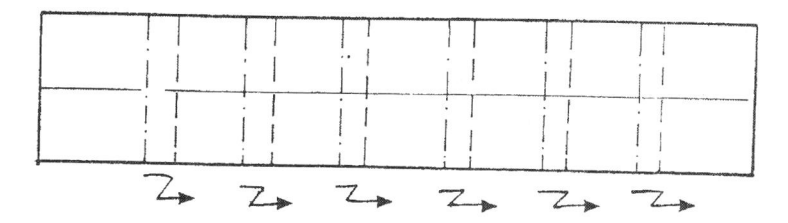

Step 2

It should now look like this. Turn the paper over.

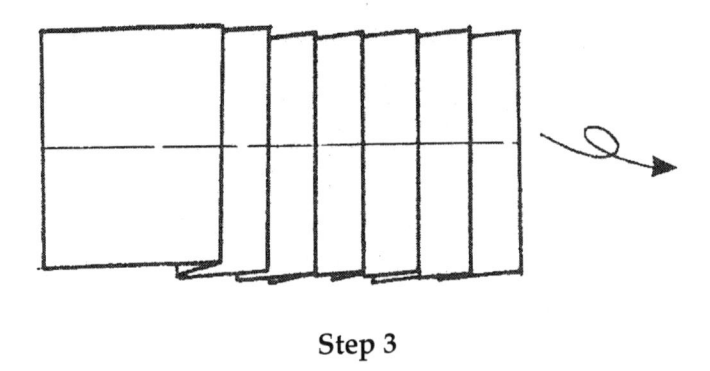

Step 3

Fold corners in to the center crease, and then fold in half.

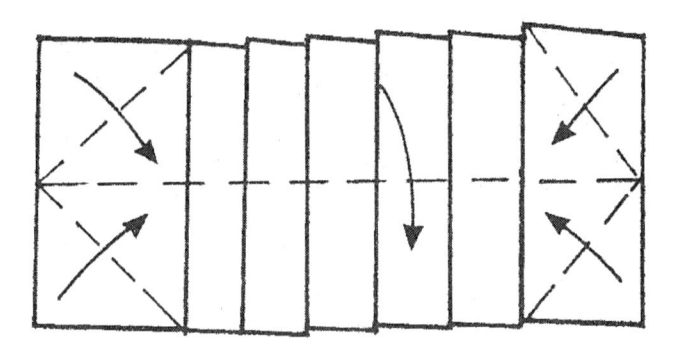

Step 4

Larger view; push in the left corner ('tail' section), and then the right corner ('nose' section). Fold back the six body segments on both sides as shown.

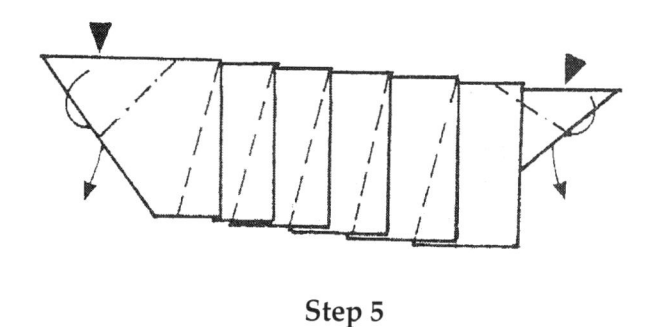

Step 5

Fold the left corner as shown on both sides, and then right corner. Fold legs back if you desire a millipede look.

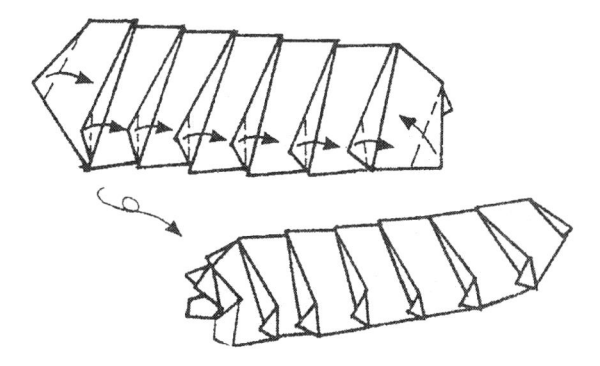

Turn the model around and you have your finished Caterpillar. You could make a long one with lots of legs for a millipede.

Scorpion

These sinister-looking critters love warm, dry areas. They belong to the arachnid group; the same group that includes spiders and ticks. Scorpions are mostly carnivorous, feeding on other insects. The poison from the stinger of some scorpion species can kill a human.

After giving birth, the female carries her young on her back for several days. Wonderfully maternal, aren't they?

This model is a simplified version. Once you have made one, try experimenting with the inside folds by slitting the outer paper layers into strips and folding out to make legs. When your skills reach an advanced level, Robert J. Lang has a nice scorpion in his book, *Origami Insects*.

Step 1

Fold a square diagonally in one direction and then unfold, and then fold up the other diagonal as shown.

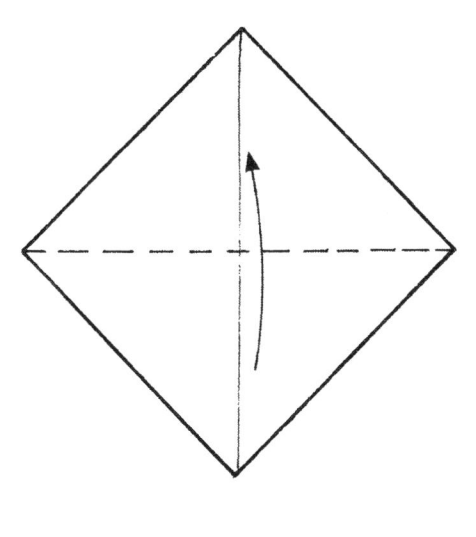

Step 2

Fold top flap to meet bottom edge.

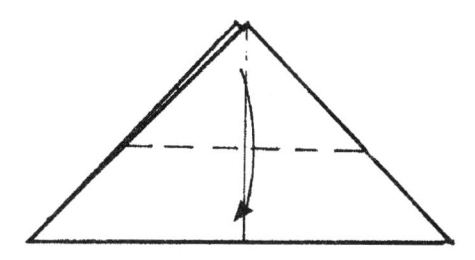

Step 3

Should look like this. Turn the paper over and then fold two rabbit-ears. To do this, first crease fold AB to meet BC, and then AC to meet BC. Bring the sides together and fold the points downwards.

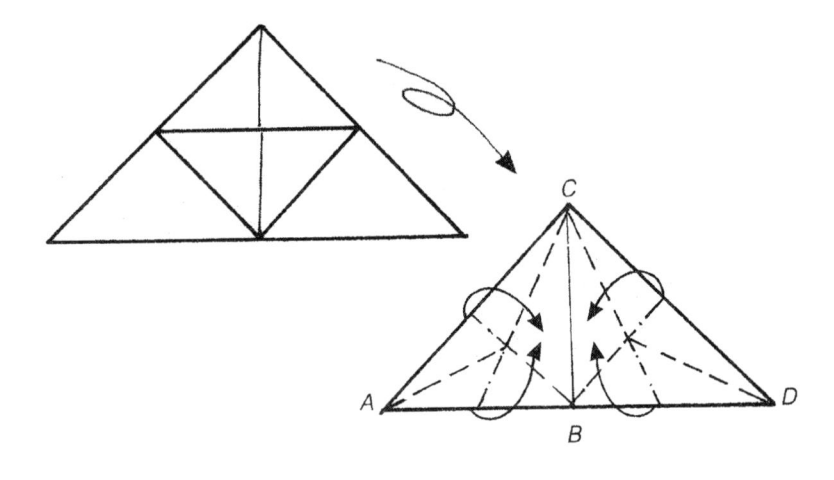

Step 4

Fold sides to meet the center crease and then stair-step fold the point four times in the approximate position shown.

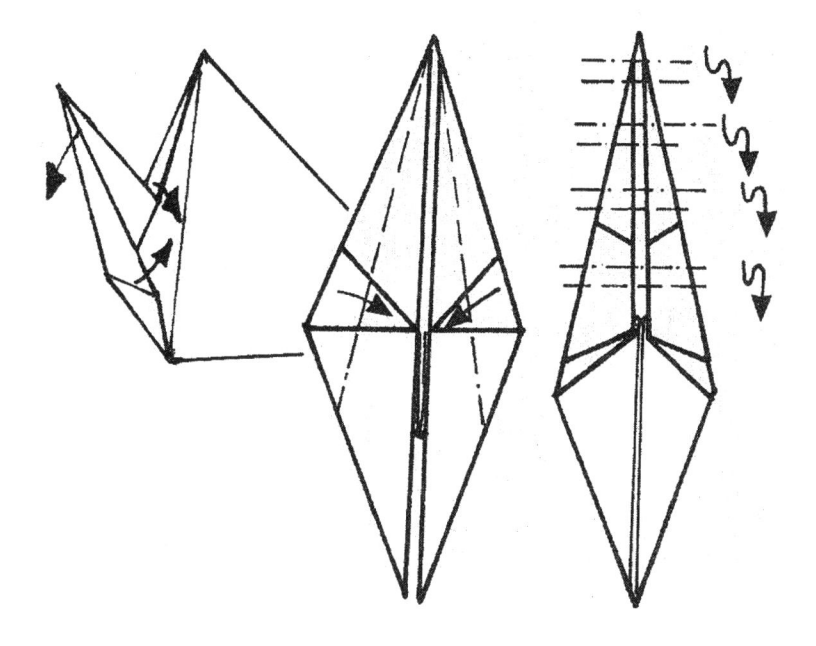

Step 5

Larger view; turn the model over. Fold up point A (top flap only). Now fold out the pincers.

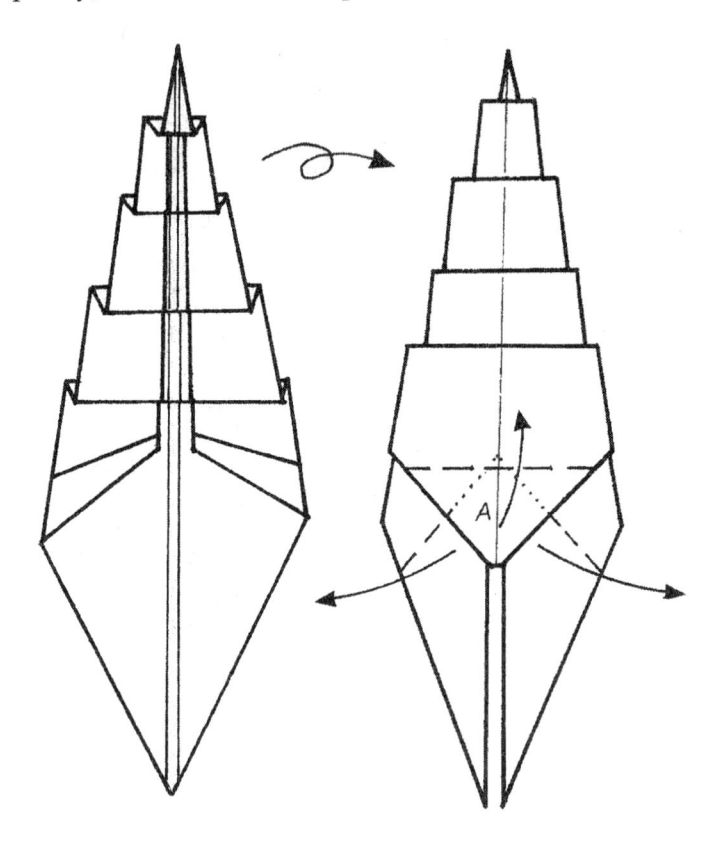

Step 6

Outside reverse fold the pincers and then mountain-fold the model in half lengthwise.

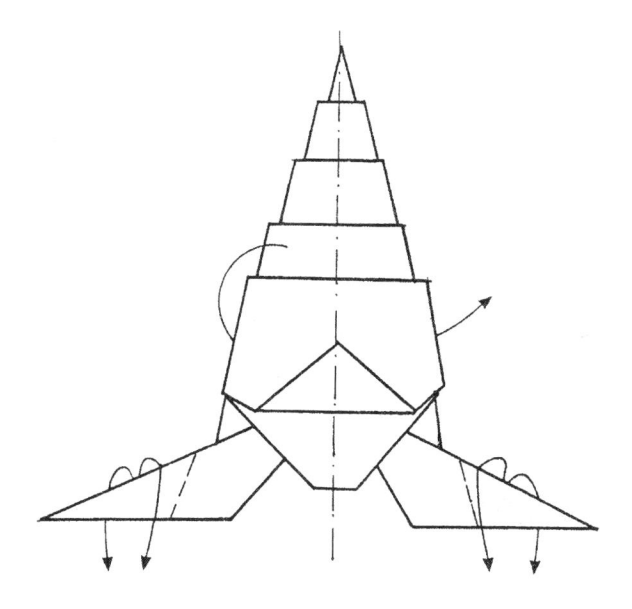

Step 7

This is a close-up side-on view of the pincer; inside reverse fold the point to make a little nipper.

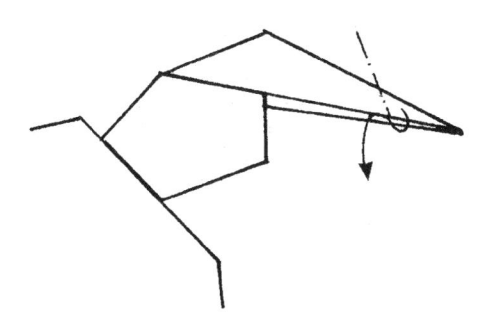

Step 8

Push in B to form the nose. While firmly holding together the head and thorax section (where indicated by the small circle) pull up the abdomen sections so that they curl to eventually point forward. Open out the pincers.

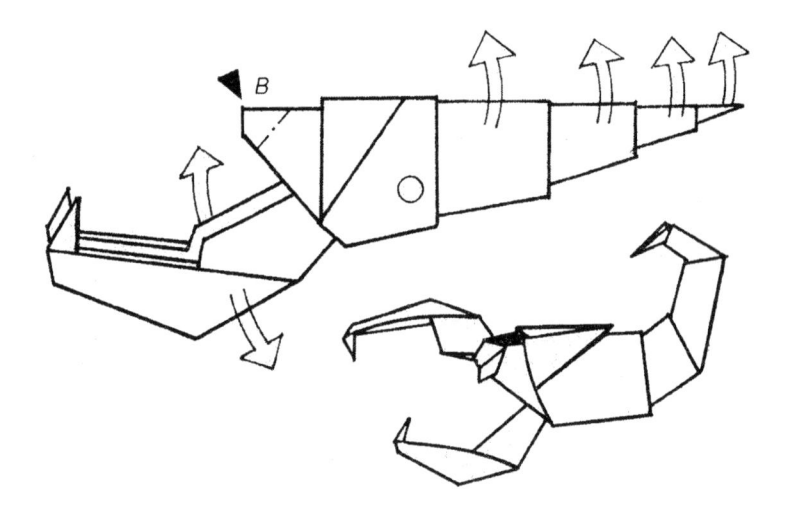

Your completed Scorpion (above); fold one out of brown or black paper and place it on the beach. No one will dare take your favorite sun-tanning spot!

Dragonfly

Dragonflies are awesome-looking insects. They feature long bodies with huge transparent wings, some with wingspans of up to 18 centimeters! Like the scorpion, dragonflies are voracious carnivores, flies and mosquitoes topping their menu.

Step 1

Begin with the Bird Base facing you upside down. Fold both the top points outwards at the angle shown. Now fold the hidden lower flap up behind.

Paper Bugs!

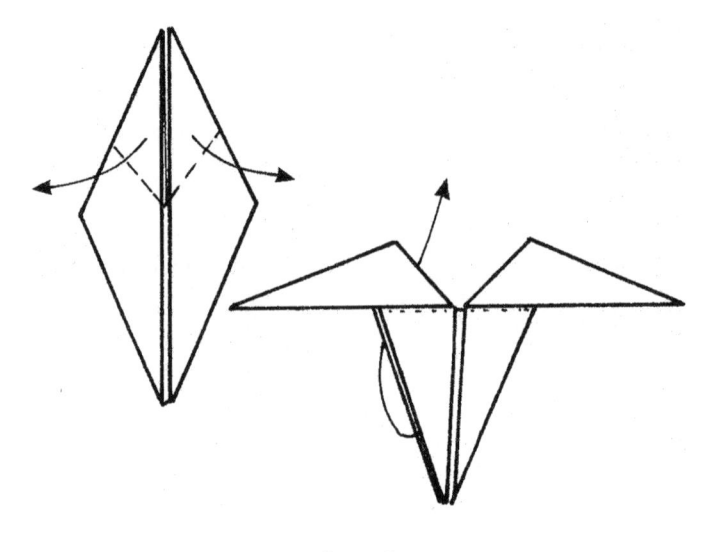

Step 2

It should look like this. Turn the model over.

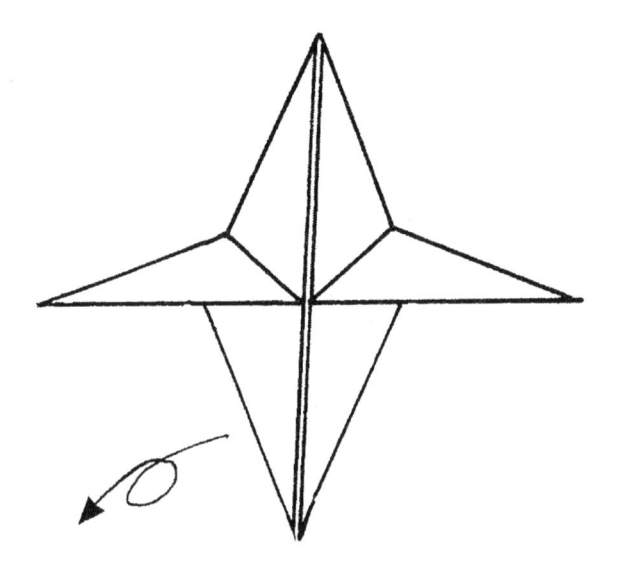

Step 3

Position the model as shown. Place your thumb under A, lifting the side upwards and into the center crease. Part of the wing folds to the right. Looking at the cut-away image, the fold is nearly complete. Flatten the fold and then repeat for the other side.

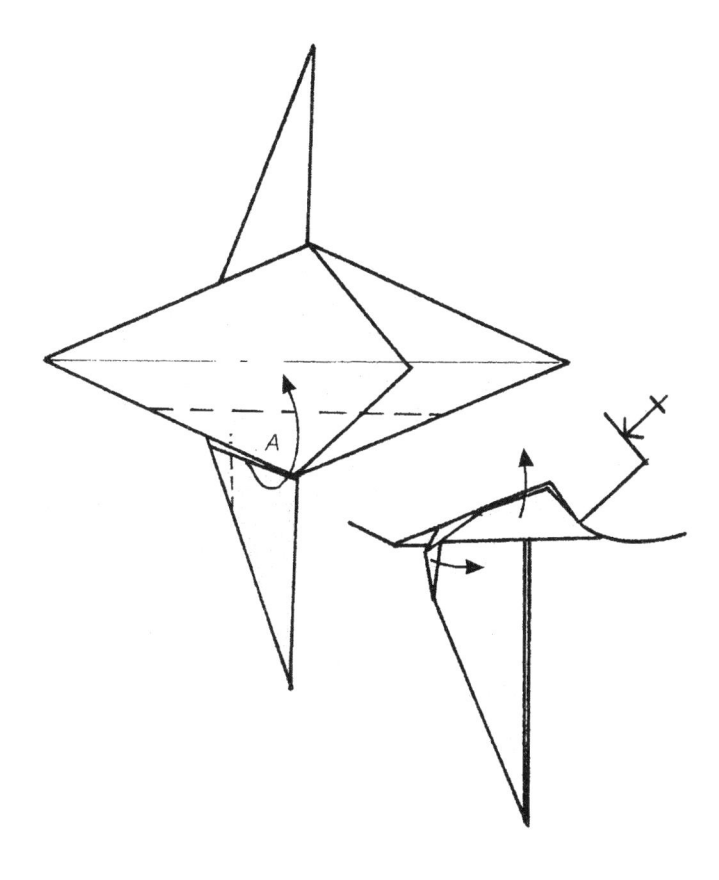

Step 4

Fold lengthwise in half.

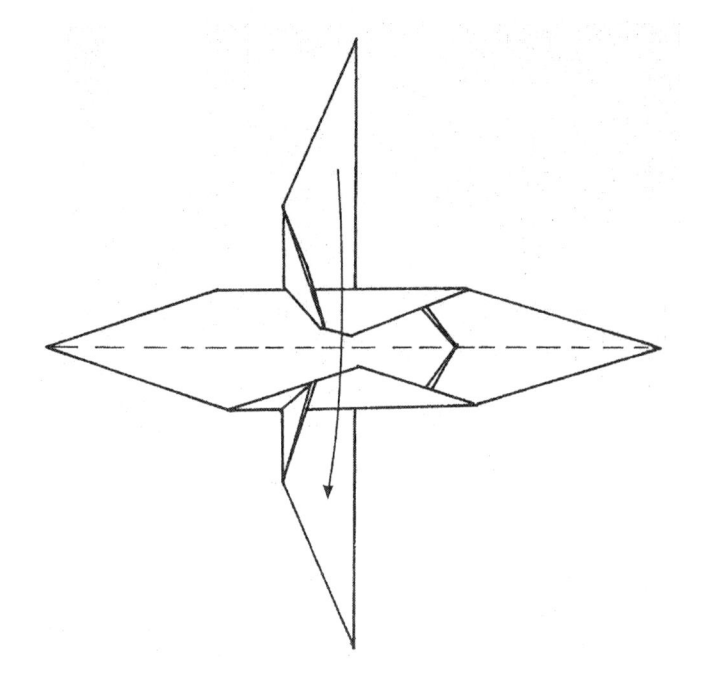

Step 5

The wings are several paper layers thick. Grab a pair of small scissors and slit open the top layer along XX and YY, then fold entire upper flap layer over to the left. Repeat for other side.

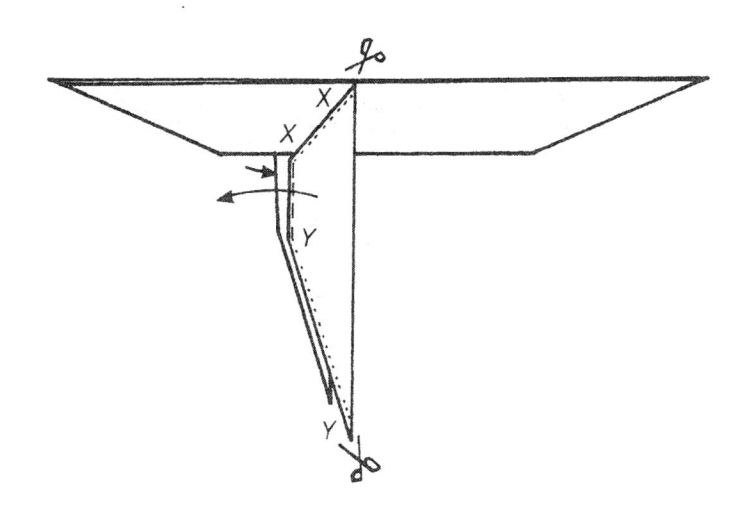

Step 6

Fold up wings along the valley fold indicated. Note hidden flaps: these pop out downwards as the wings are folded up. *Do not fold them too!*

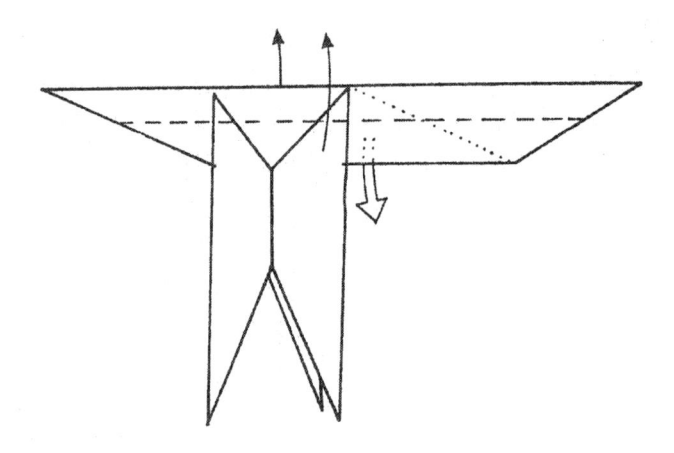

Step 8

Fold behind the tail end flaps. Fold the wings down, and then open out the center of the model and have it facing you as shown in the next step (looking down).

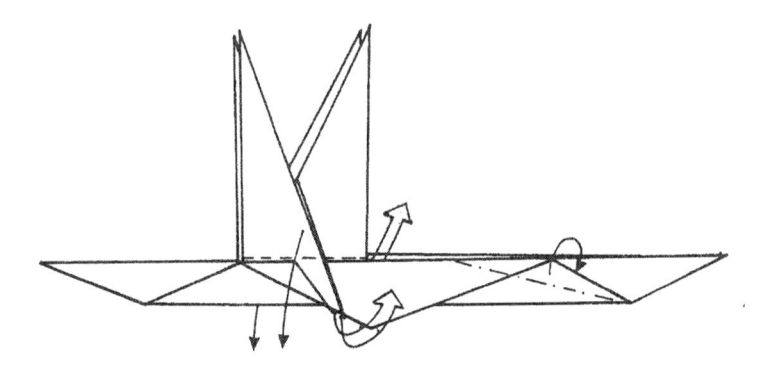

Step 9

Looking down on your model from above, with it opened out, fold up the loose points of the new wings.

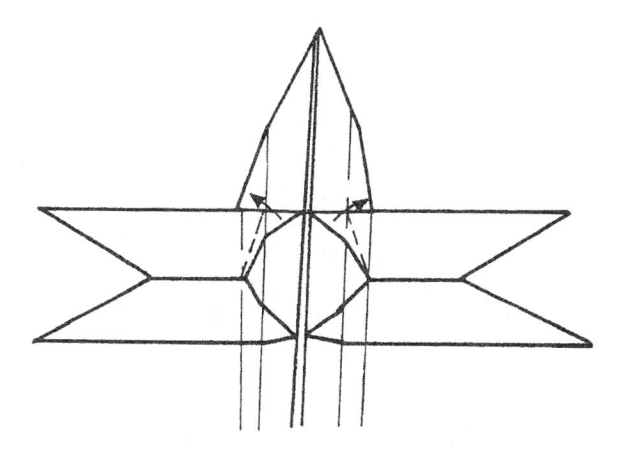

Step 10

Bring in the sides by refolding the valley fold made in Step 6 and then stair-step fold the head section. This will lock the front wings in place.

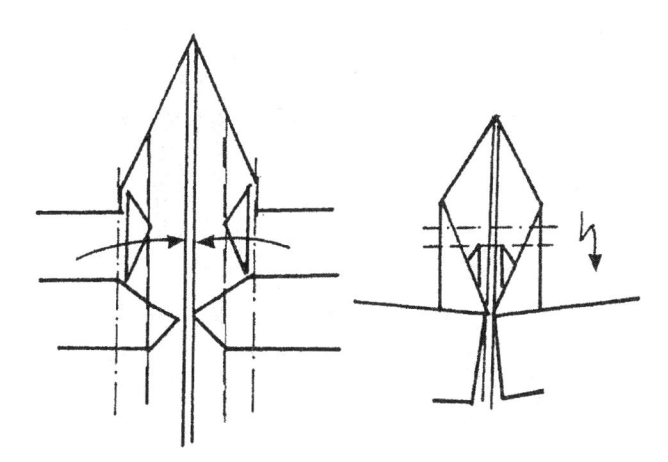

Step 12

Fold behind in half along the length of the body.

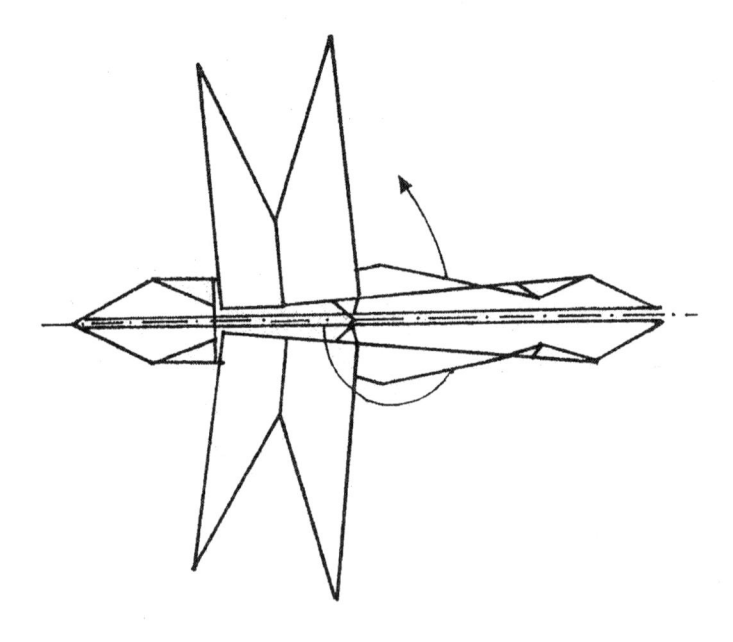

Step 13

Have the model face you as shown. Lift up the wings so that they are horizontal. Reverse stair-step fold the head, noting angle of folds.

Now tuck the point of the nose inside the head to complete your dragonfly.

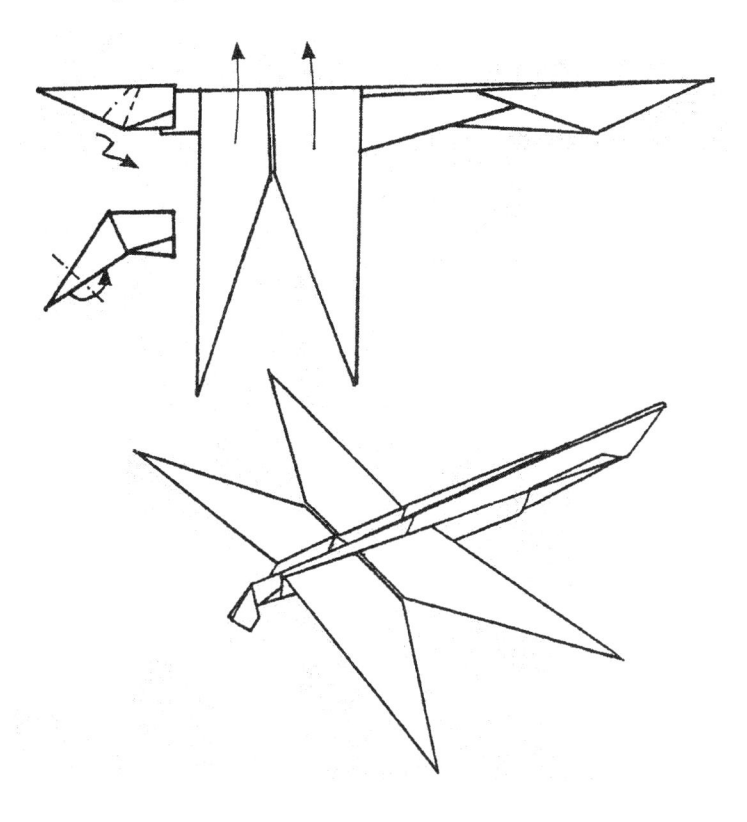

Snail

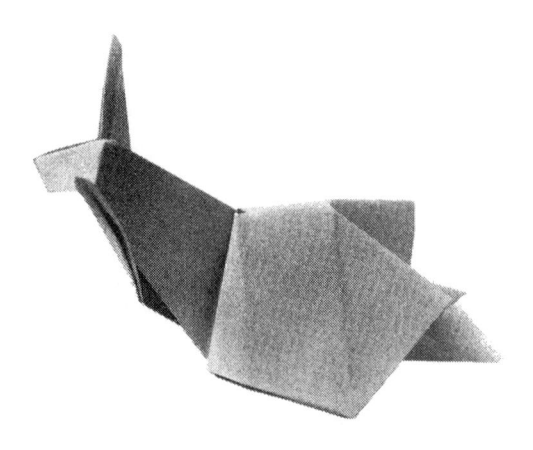

These gastropod mollusks come in all sizes on land and fresh and salt water. The retractable sensory head tentacles of a snail look like eyes. They do have simple eyes, which come as a second pair of tentacles closer to the head. The snail is a well-known part of French cooking (escargot). However, imagine being served a giant African snail; could you eat it all in one go?

I was lucky enough to be hunting real land snails near a beach with a friend from the local museum. I found an interesting woodland snail and my malacology friend soon realized it was a previously undiscovered species. It is now named, Meridolum Pommerhelix *carmelae*.

Step 1

Begin with the Bird Base. Open points facing upwards and fold up the lower flaps on both sides. Now, fold down both points in the approximate position shown.

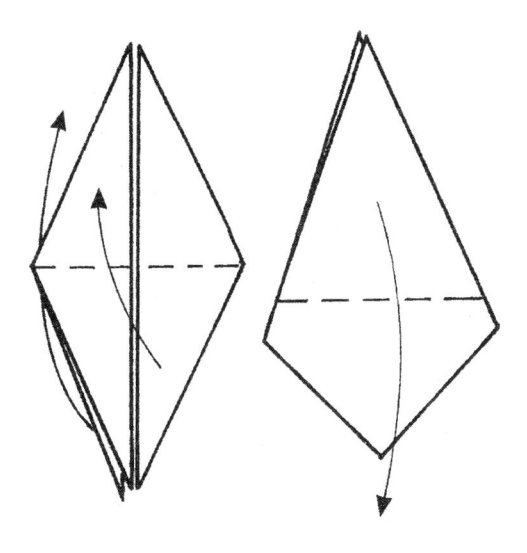

Step 2

Fold the down-pointing flaps up where shown.

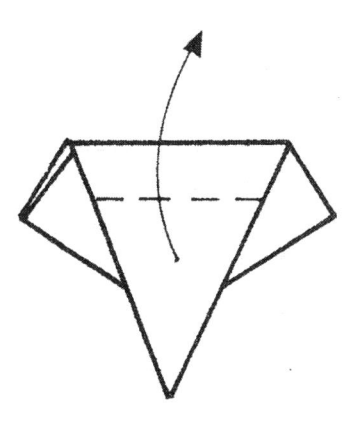

Step 3

Fold down only the uppermost flap where shown and then fold model lengthwise in half.

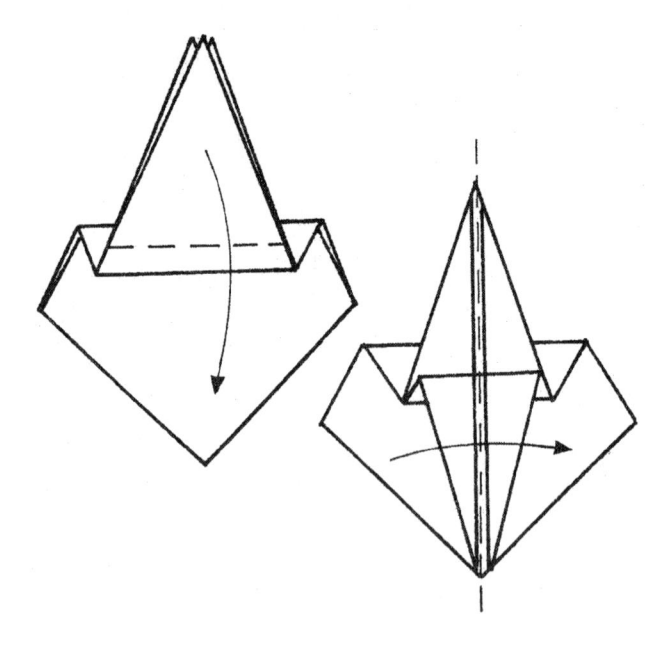

Step 4

Facing you as shown, hold the snail's body firmly (on the area marked with a small circle) and pull down the hidden tail X. Now pull up entire head section, after which you then pull down the inside points of the head section.

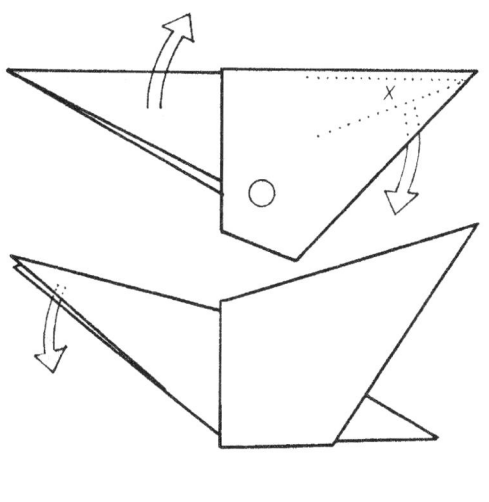

Step 5

Fold up the tentacles. For the shell, do an inverse mountain and then valley fold.

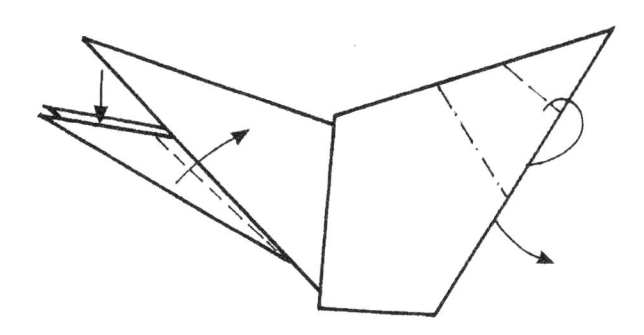

Step 6

Head section is shown at left, tail section at right (where you just did the inverse folds. For the head, tuck the nose point under. Reverse stair-step fold the head section, carefully noting the angle of the valley and mountain folds. Angle out the tentacles if you wish, and snub the points a little with your finger tips to make tiny eyes.

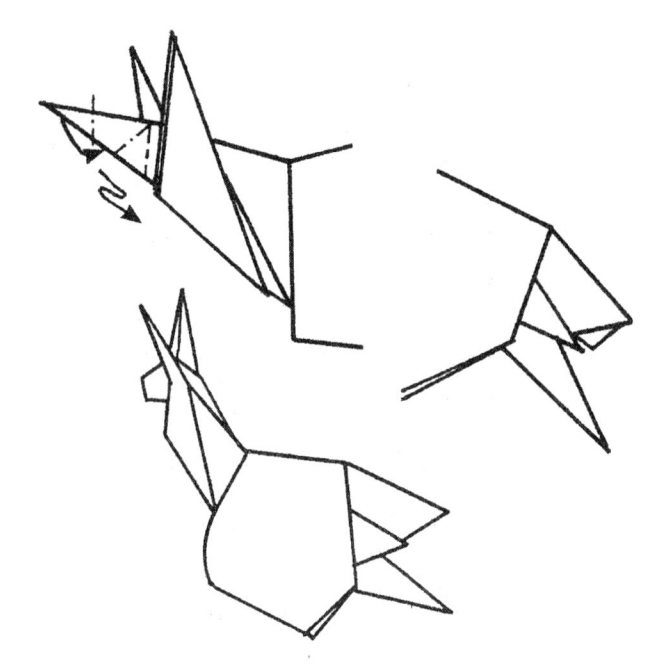

Your completed snail is shown above (lower left image). Don't let it loose in the vegetable garden. My friend Pierre has two of these on the counter of his French restaurant with the word, 'Manifique' written on each one.

Cockroach

These detestable creatures are, so I am told, actually quite tasty when added to a Waldorf salad, so long as you don't know what you're eating. 'They taste like soft Walnuts' someone once said. I hope to never confirm if this is true.

There are around 3500 species of cockroach scampering across the world's floors and forests. They don't fly much and prefer the night hours for eating and the warmth of human company. My house doesn't have cockroaches; the big hairy spiders get them.

Step 1

Begin with the Preliminary Base. Open out the front right flap, noting valley and mountain folds.

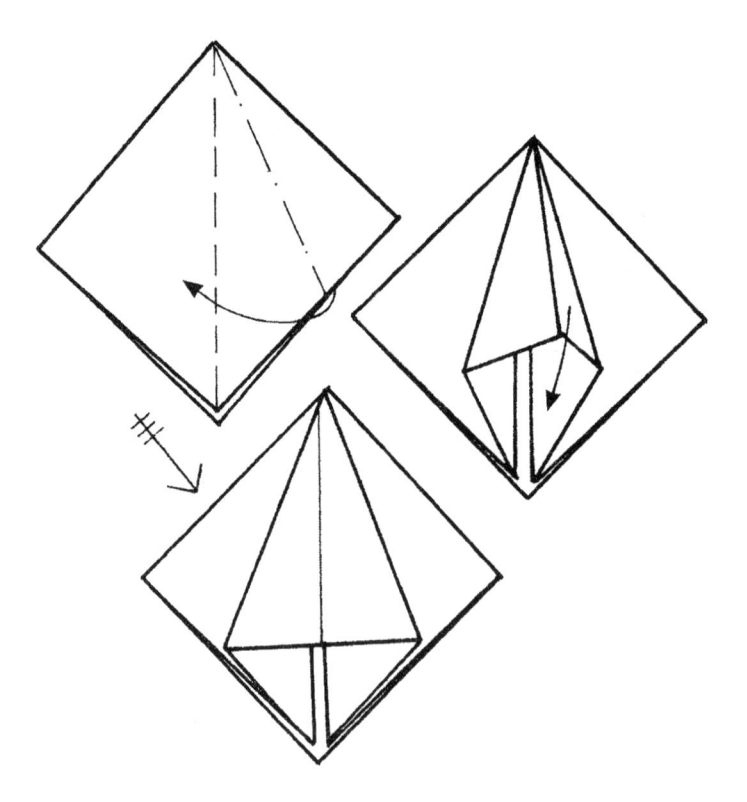

The second image shows the fold before flattening. Flatten the fold. The third image shows the completed fold. Repeat this procedure for the other three sides.

Step 2

Crease-fold the sides along lines AC and BD and then crease-fold entire top section along AB. Lift the flap upwards in the same manner as for the bird base and flatten the fold.

It should look like the image at right. Again, repeat this procedure for the other points.

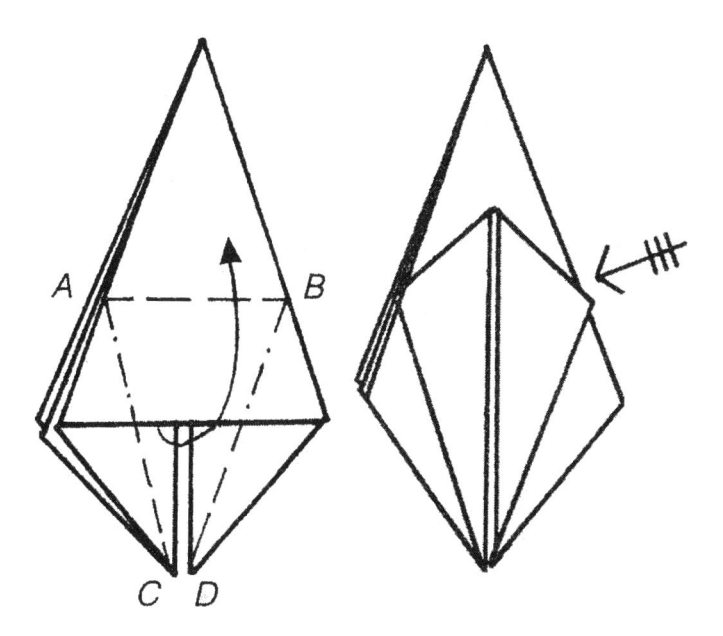

Step 3

Flip the front left flap to the right and flip the back-right flap to the left. Fold sides of front flap in to center crease.

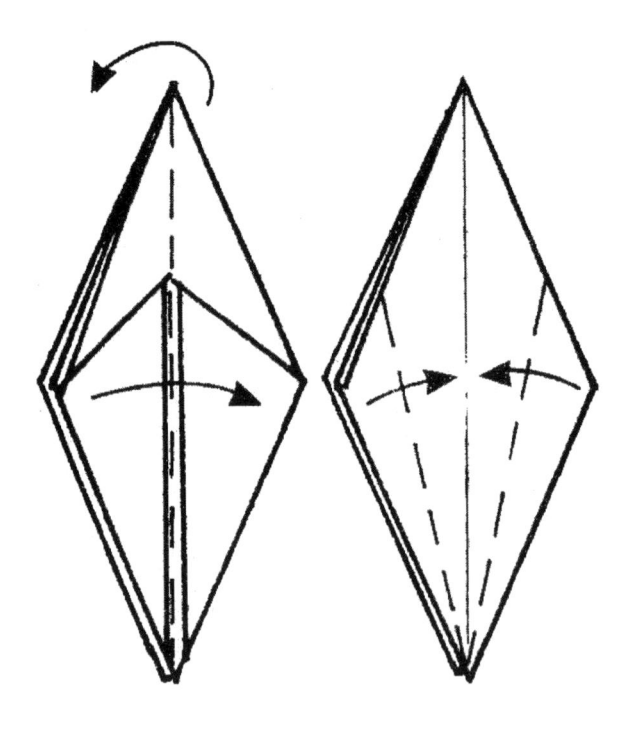

Step 4

(Left image) Fold bottom point up to meet top point. Repeat for the opposite side.

(Middle image) Now flip front left section to the right, at the same time flipping back-right flap to the left.

(Right-hand image) Place your thumb and finger at the center of the diamond where the circle indicates and hold firmly. Pull the top inside points outwards.

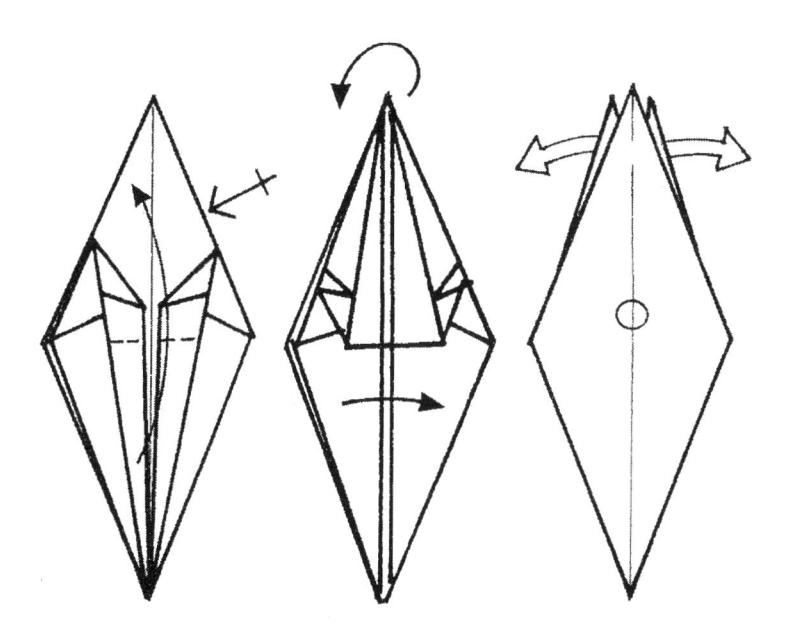

Step 5

(Uppermost image) Fold the sides in and fold one end in.

(Lowermost image) Stair-step the head section, creasing well. Fold center points outwards. Now turn the model over.

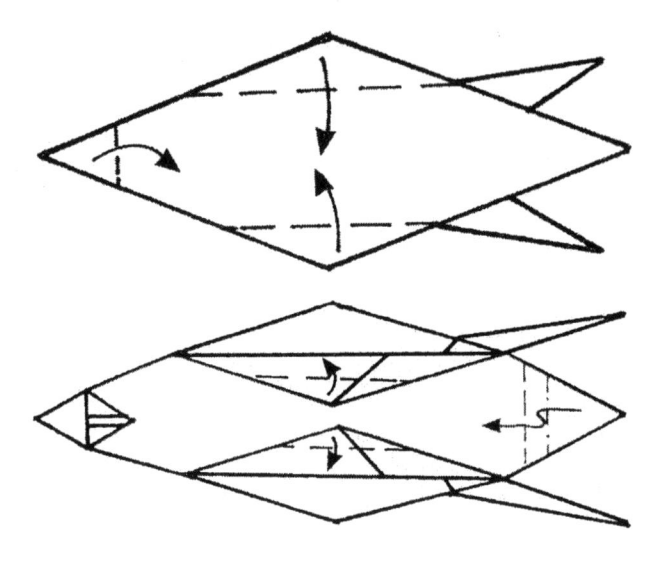

Step 6

Fold antennae outwards and fold the point between the antennae under to form the head. Now snip through the upper flap from left point to meet the center crease of the model. This will form the wings.

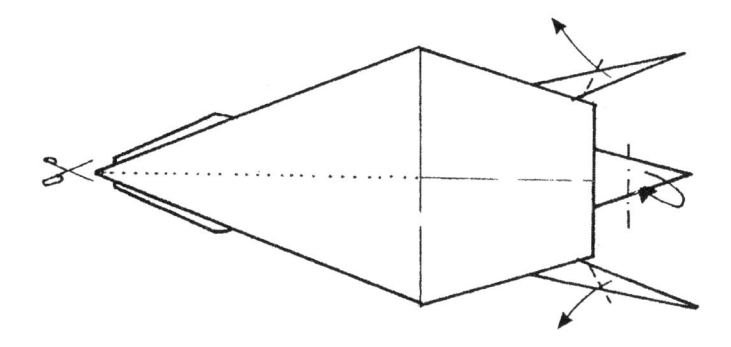

Step 7

(Left image) Fold up both wings.

(Right image) Fold back the wings at the angle shown.

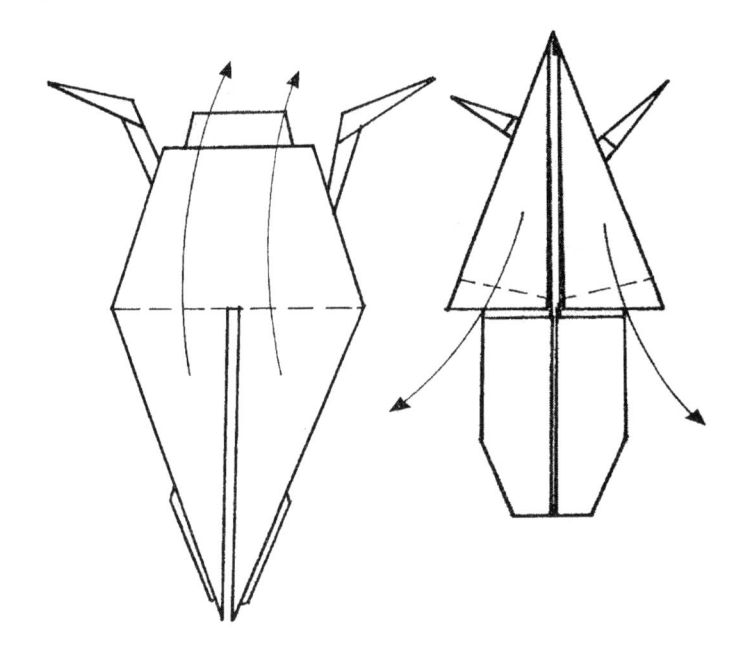

Step 8

Fold the wing joins under to round out the creature. Crease-fold the creature lengthwise in half and round out the entire body.

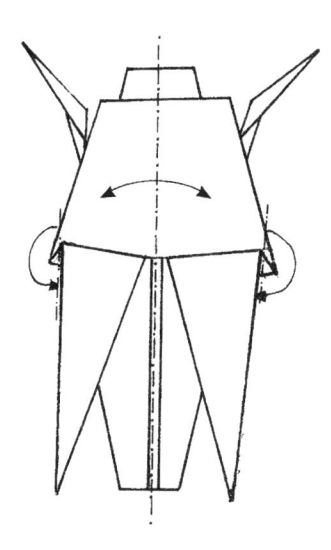

The completed Cockroach is shown below.

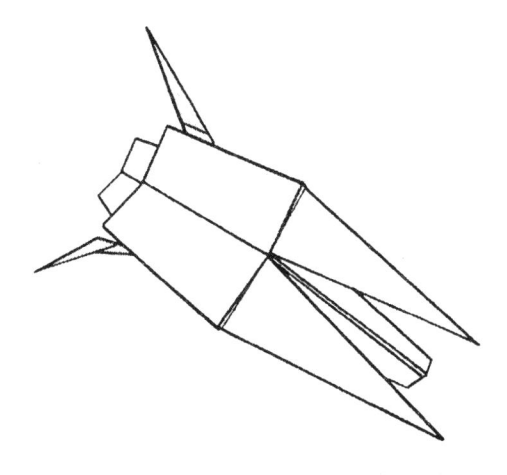

Butterfly

With all the grotesque critters I've duplicated in paper, it's now time for something more appealing. Butterflies start out as the more homely caterpillar. They hungrily chew through countless leaves before developing a hard carapace. From a chrysalis, they struggle into the world, unfolding their exquisite multi-colored wings.

By using stiff patterned paper, a real-looking butterfly can be made with little effort.

Step 1

Begin with a square diagonally crease folded in half both ways. Fold back in half as shown.

Snip the top flap with scissors along the center crease and then turn the model over.

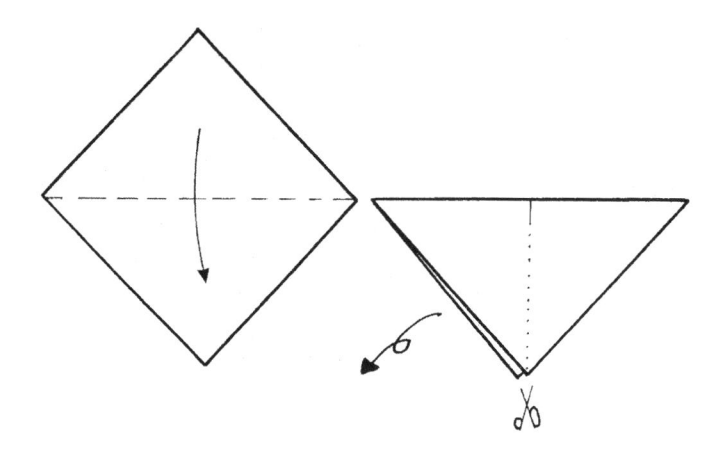

Step 2

Fold the corners in to meet the center crease, and then flip out the previously-cut flaps from behind.

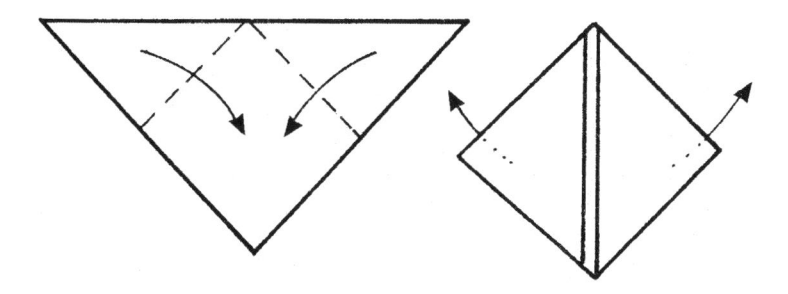

Step 3

Fold the cut flaps into the center crease.

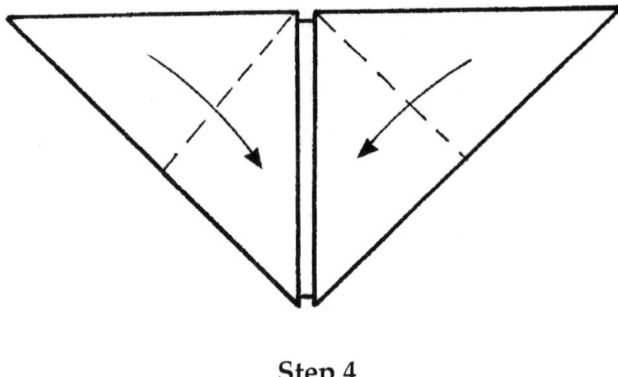

Step 4

Rabbit-ear the top left flap and as shown in the second image fold the point up. Repeat for the right-hand flap.

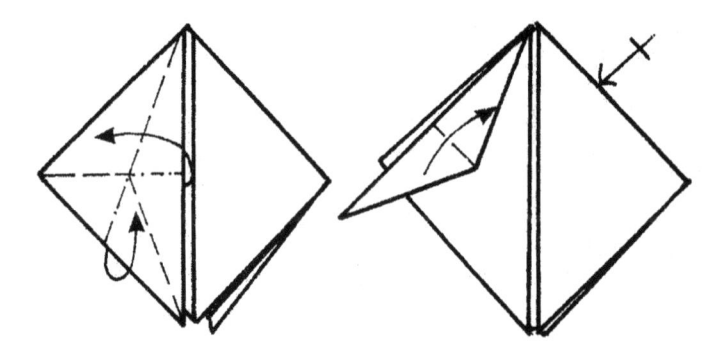

Step 5

With scissors, snip the bottom flap in two, cutting up to the center of the model (AB). Fold the top two flaps out as shown.

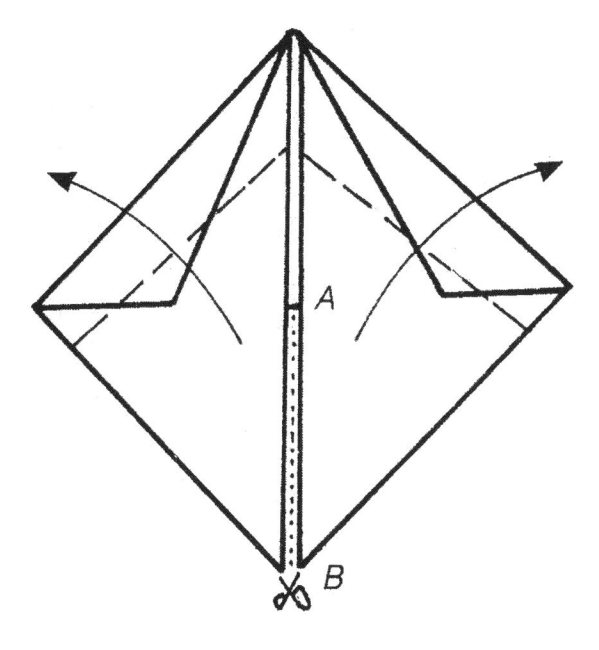

Step 6

Fold model in half and swing around so that it faces you side on.

Fold wings up in approximate position shown in the right-hand image. The two left points inside will pop downwards. These will become the antennae.

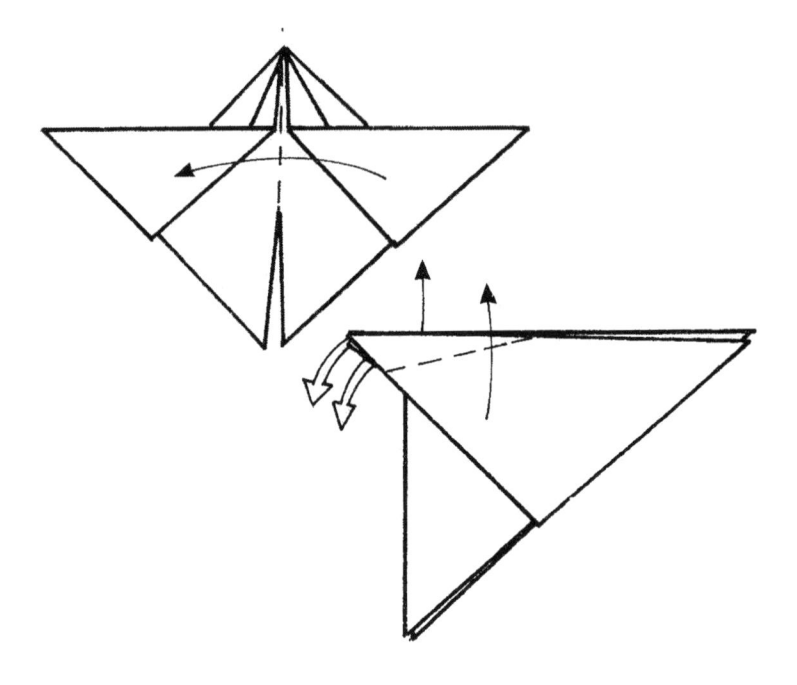

Step 7

Fold these two points up to form the antennae.

(Upper right close-up image) Fold down again.

(Lower right close-up image) Fold up points again to make a finer point.

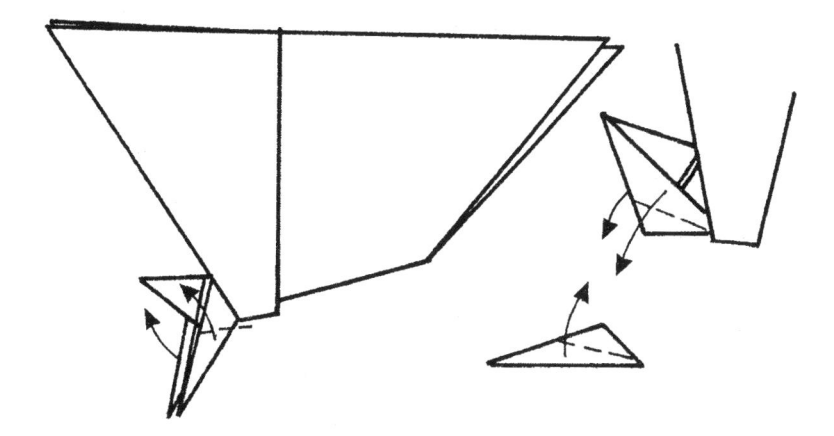

Step 8

Fold wings down where shown.

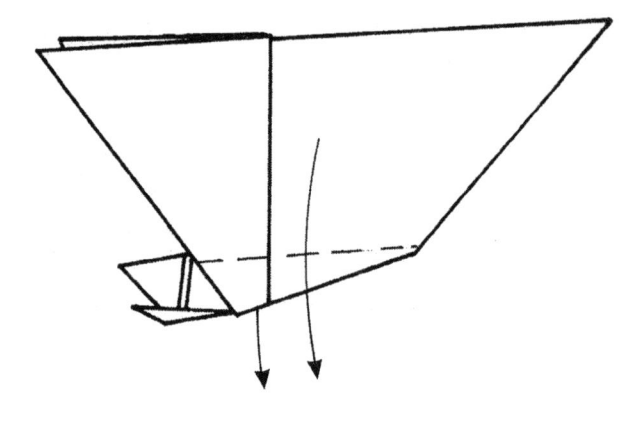

Step 9

The model shown here is upside down. Tuck back the front head section (point B) to seal the body together, and then turn the model over.

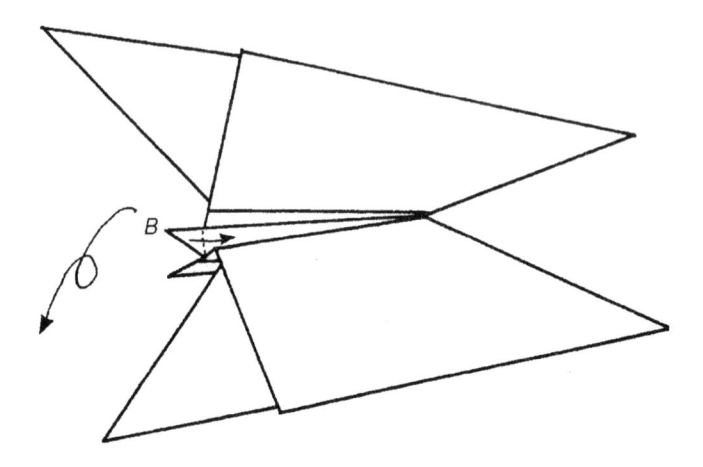

Step 10

Your completed Butterfly is shown below. This model actually flies! Holding the rear wings, gently let go of your butterfly with a slight forward motion. It will glide, somewhat erratically (like a butterfly). Perhaps if you made a large one out of stiff paper and attached a reel of string you could have a butterfly kite.

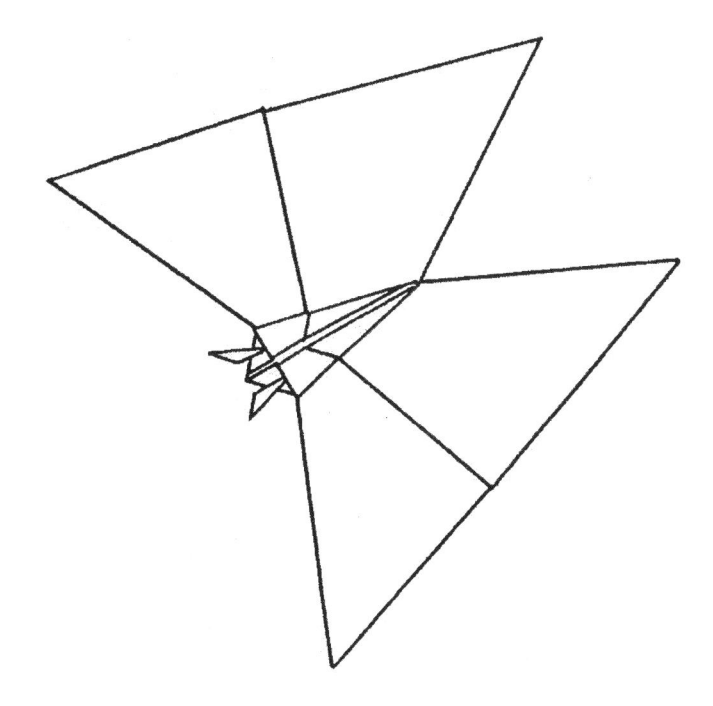

Bee

Here's one for your honey! Bees have highly specialized tongues for feeding on the pollen and nectar of many different flowers. This enables them to make honey as well as to cross-pollinate plants. The social structure of bees is well developed and consists of male drones, workers (infertile female bees) and a fertile queen bee.

Bee stings are painful and some people are allergic to them, so making a paper bee is the best alternative to catching a real one.

Step 1

Repeat steps 1 to 3 of the Dragonfly. Stair-step fold four times as indicated. Inverse fold the wingtips.

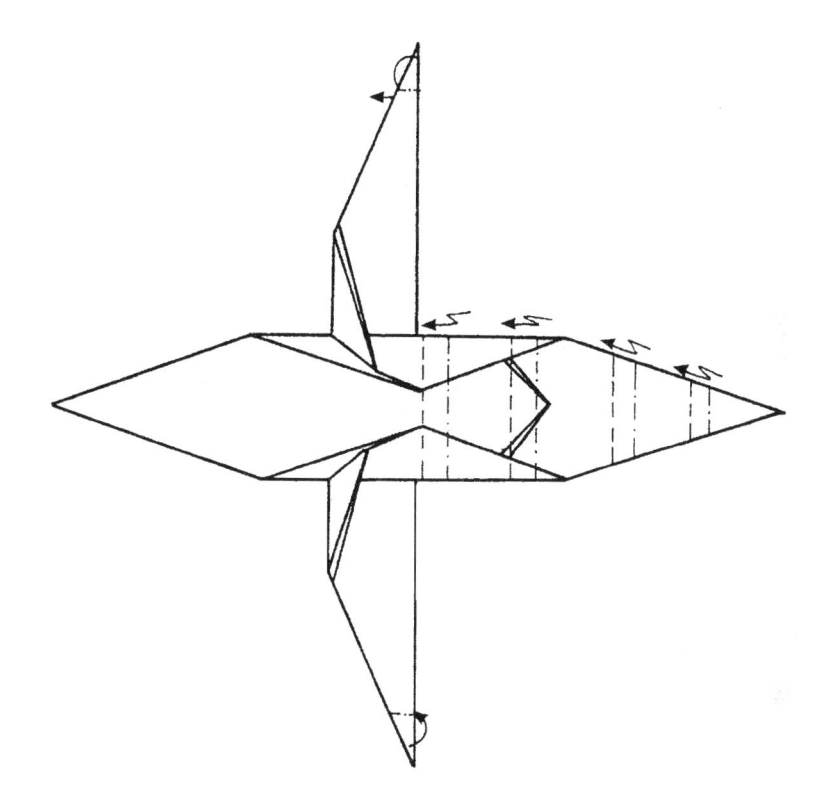

Step 2

Noting stinger section, fold sides in to make a fine point and then fold the model in half.

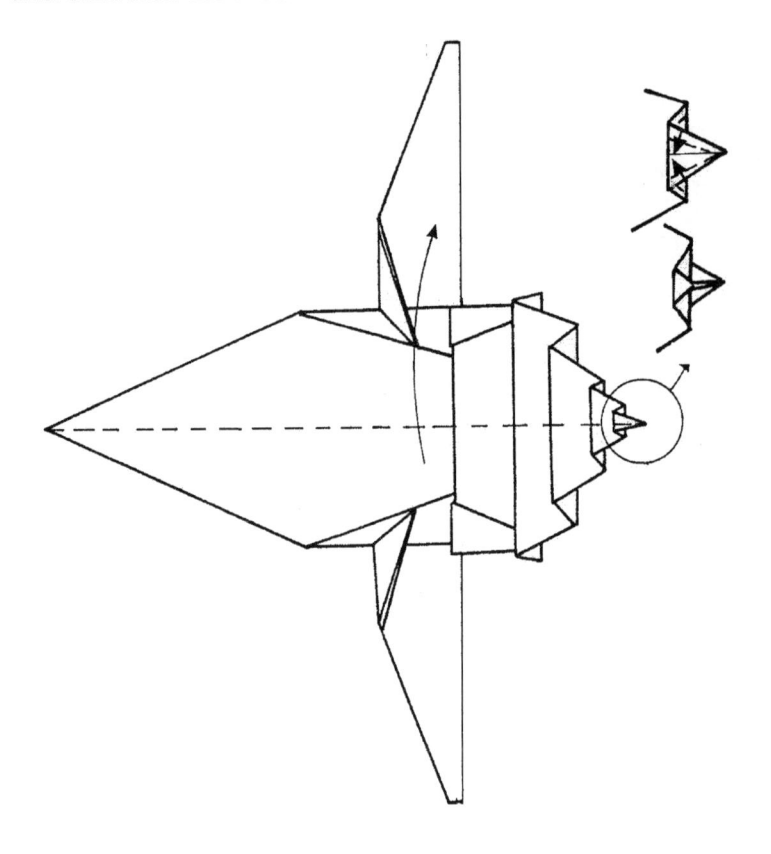

Step 3

Inverse fold the head section. Hold model firmly at the base of its wings and pull down the body section.

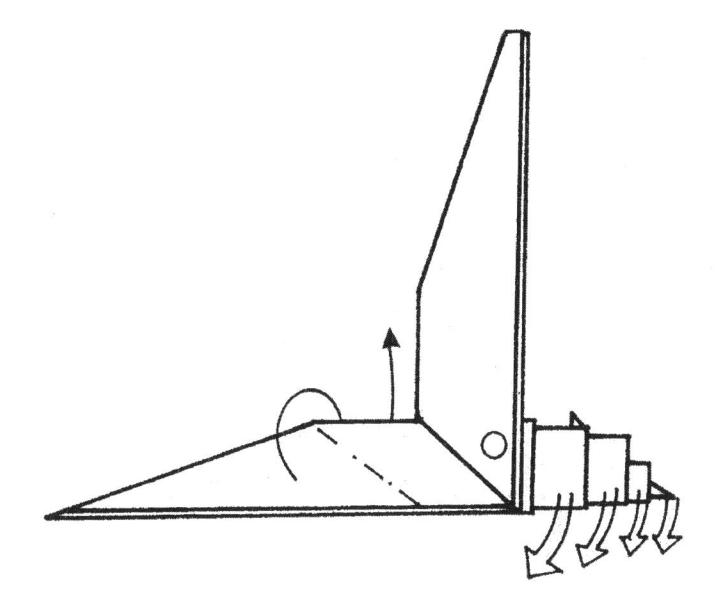

Step 4

Inverse fold the head downwards and crease-fold the wings. For the head section, reverse fold down and reverse fold the point back and up slightly.

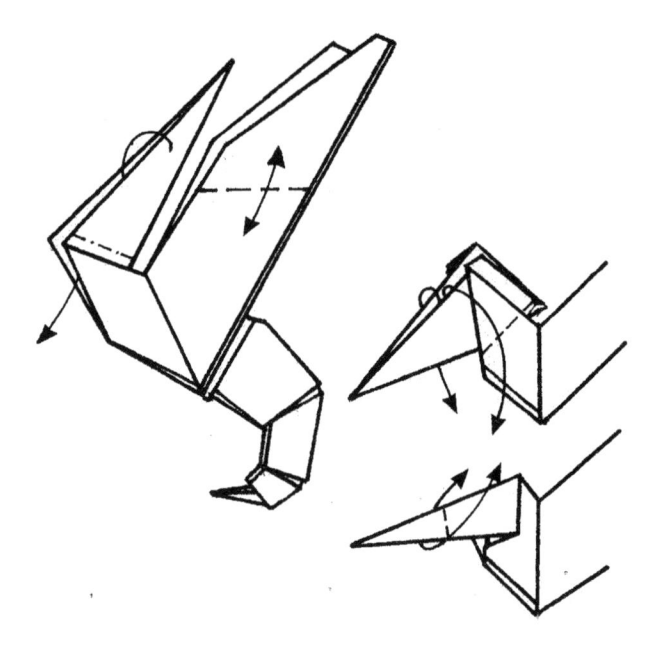

Step 5

(Left image) Now snip part way through the head top flap and fold out the two antennae.

(Right image) Reverse stair-step fold the head itself (noting angle of fold lines).

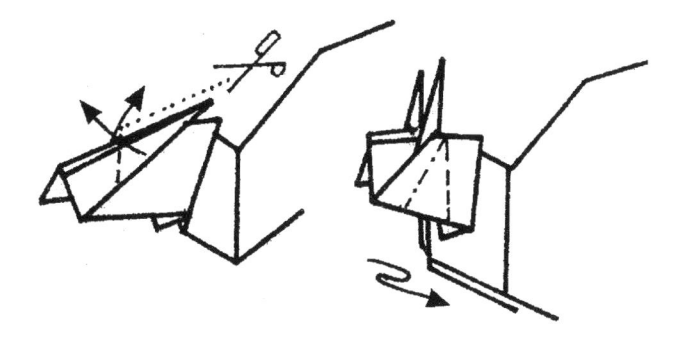

Step 6

Your completed Bee is shown below. If you wish, snip apart the wings to create the more realistic four wing effect.

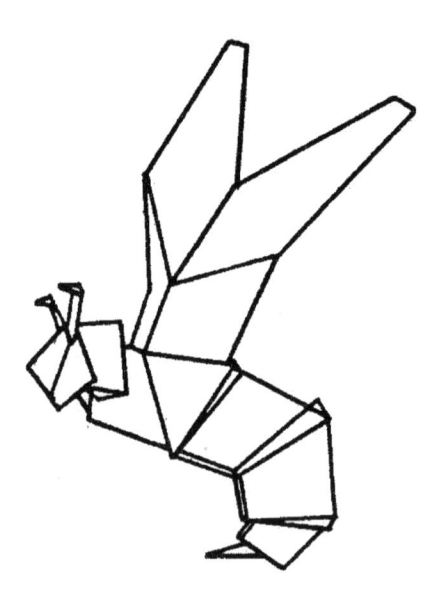

Fly

Flies can be a nuisance at any time, no matter how small be it a house fly or fruit fly. This model, being folded using large paper by comparison may as well be a blow-fly (Calliphoridae). Such flies often lay their eggs in dung and rotting meat.

While some come in interesting colors, let's face it, they're not an insect you could get attached to even though they have no problem attaching themselves to you!

Step 1

Begin with the Preliminary Base.

(Top image) Fold the bottom point up in half, unfold, then fold bottom point to new crease and fold up again.

(Lower left image) Fold the two sides of the top flap behind. It should look like it does in the lower right image. Turn the model over.

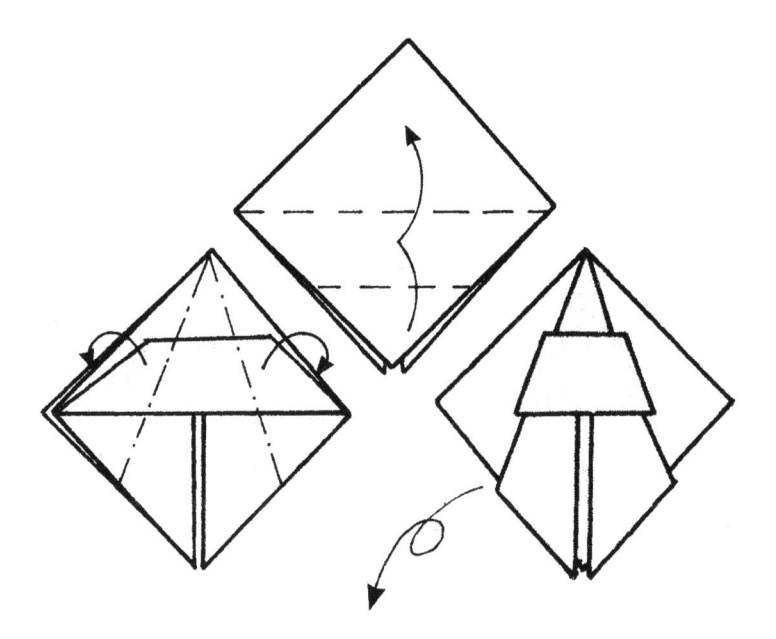

Step 2

(Upper left image) Fold this side of the model as if you were folding the Bird Base.

(Right hand image) Snip through the middle of the top fold, and then fold the two points down.

(Lower image) Larger view; fold out these points at the angles shown.

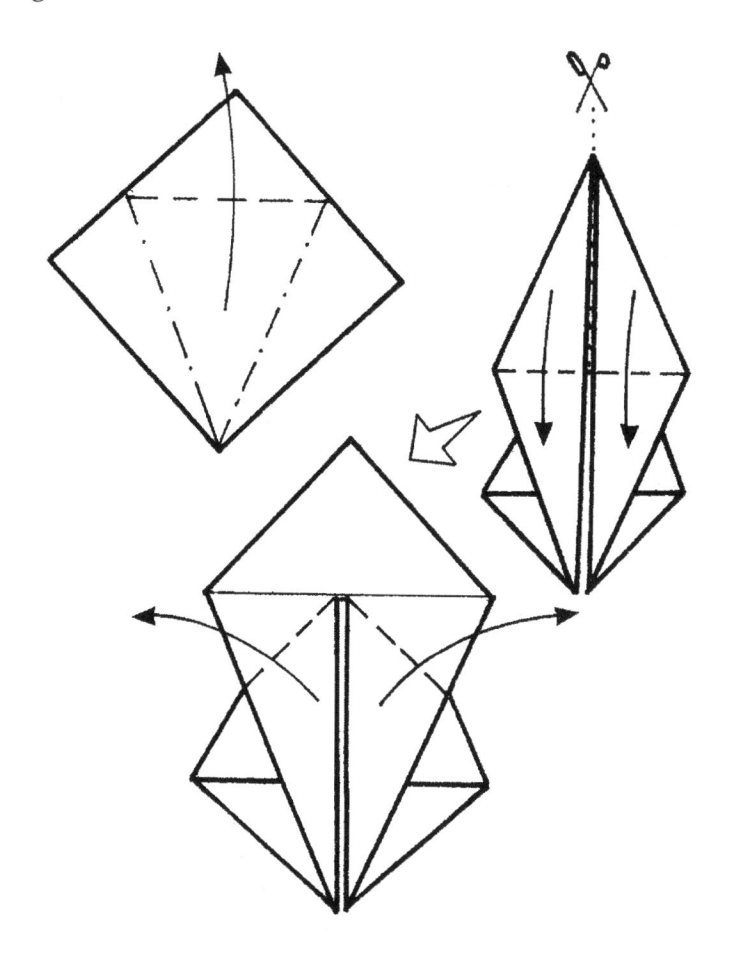

Step 3

Fold up the edges. Note lower point. Snip at the folds to make two new points.

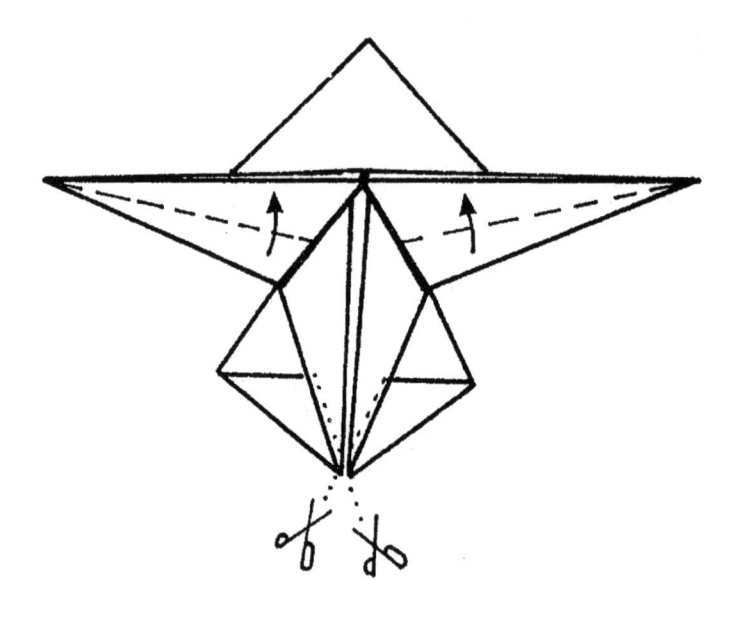

Step 4

(Left image) Fold the new lower left point out to the left along AA and then fold in the entire left 'leg' section to the right along BB.

(Right-hand image) Larger view; snip the folded edge of the top paper layer of this leg along CC, and then fold the top leg to left. Fold bottom left leg in to narrow it. Finally, inverse fold the bottom-most left point at a 45-degree angle.

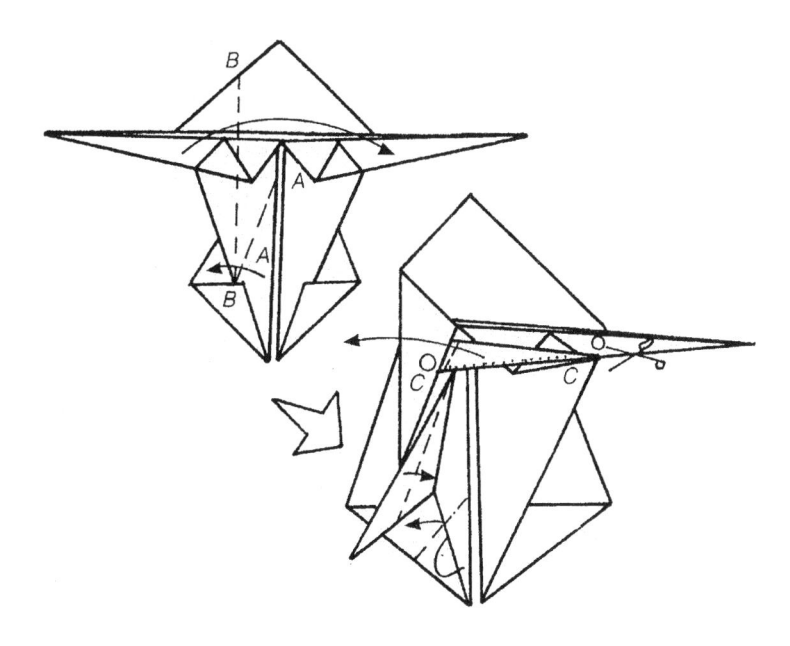

Step 5

(Left image section) Fold the remaining leg over to the center left. Repeat step 5 for the right-hand side.

(Right-hand image) Do a stair-step fold on the head section. Fold forward the feet on the front legs. Fold backwards the feet for the middle legs. Now valley crease-fold the entire body lengthwise and round out the body. Turn the model over.

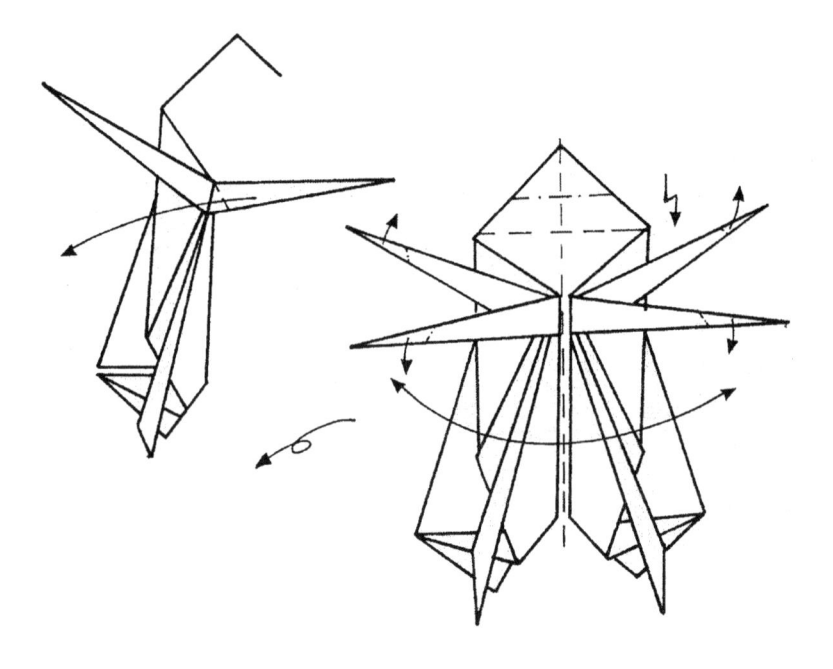

Step 6

Your completed Fly is shown below. This is one big mother of a fly. By rounding out the head and wings (folding corners in slightly) and modifying the leg positions, this model could also double as a cicada.

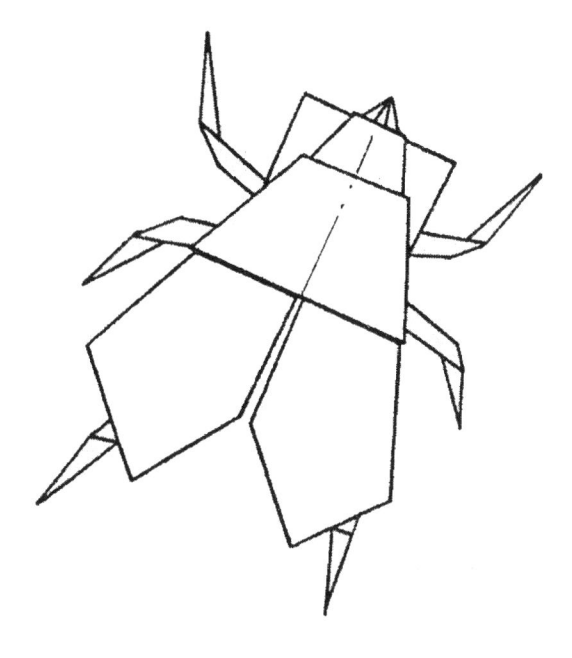

Spider

I like spiders. My Mom often reminds me about the pet tarantula I had when I was six years old. According to her, it used to climb onto my hand to take a piece of meatloaf for dinner (although they usually eat insects and sometimes mice and small lizards). I have no recollection of this event at all. :)

Spiders can have up to eight eyes, and females are usually larger than males. Sometimes after mating the female will kill the male and eat him. So much for equality!

This model could also be a tick or even a crab with minor modification. It is a simple spider; the head section can easily be modified to include pincers by stair-step folding the head point and then slitting the paper at the point down a centimeter or so to make two pincers.

Step 1

Begin with the Preliminary Base. Open out the front right flap and fold to the left. Repeat for other three sides.

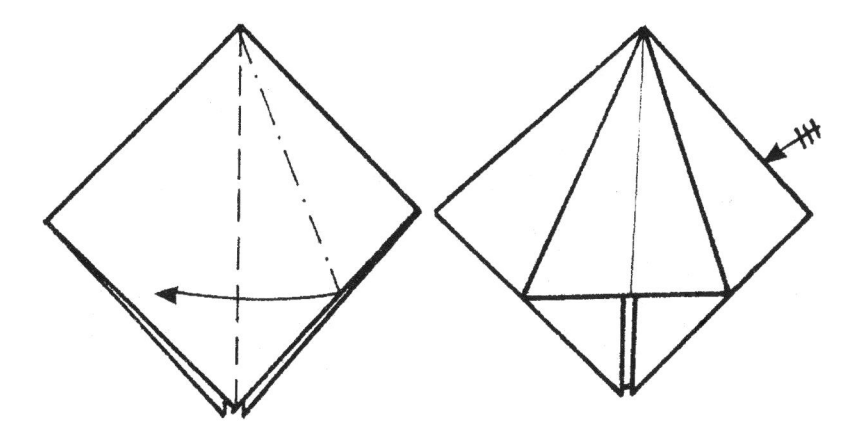

Step 2

(Left image) Crease-fold the sides along the lines AC and BD. Now crease-fold entire top section along AB. Lift the flap upwards in the same manner as for the Bird Base and flatten the fold.

(Right-hand image) Flip flap A down. Repeat for all other sides. Flip the front left flap to the right and back-right flap to the left.

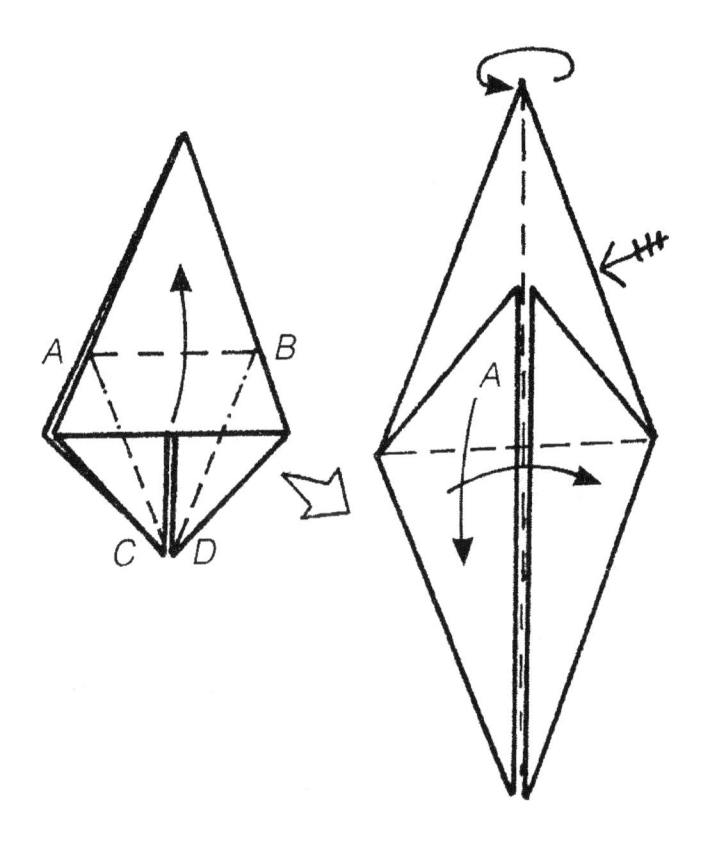

Step 3

(Top image) Fold sides in as shown and repeat all around.

(Lower image) Now cut through the bottom flap to center of the model. Repeat for all sides. Fold in the lower edges.

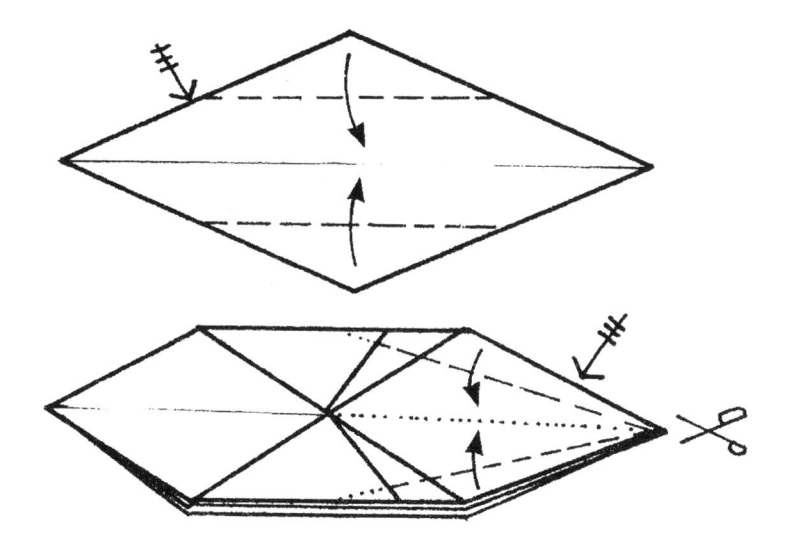

Step 4

(Top image) Fold legs out where shown. Flip the sides and repeat the procedure all round.

(Lower image) Manipulate the top legs so that they are generally pointing up. Fold lower legs inside and outwards, pointing down. Turn the model over.

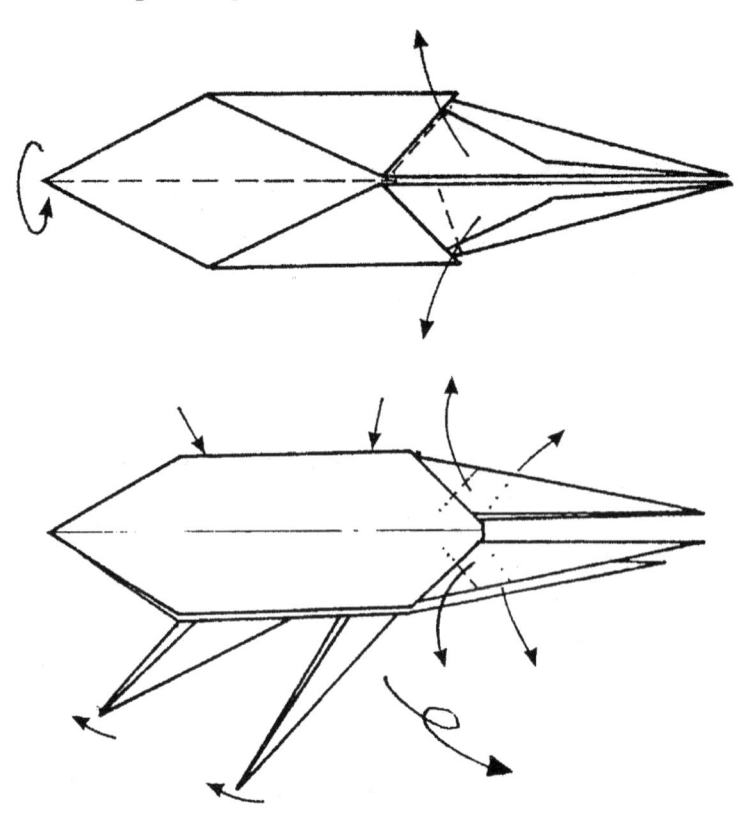

Step 5

Your critter should look something like this. In this shape it could easily be one of the long-bodied hunting spiders.

Also note the back legs; these could be slit to make another pair and the front legs could be modified to be pincers.

That's the beauty of origami; you could make nearly anything you like! For our spider, fold the abdomen section to the left.

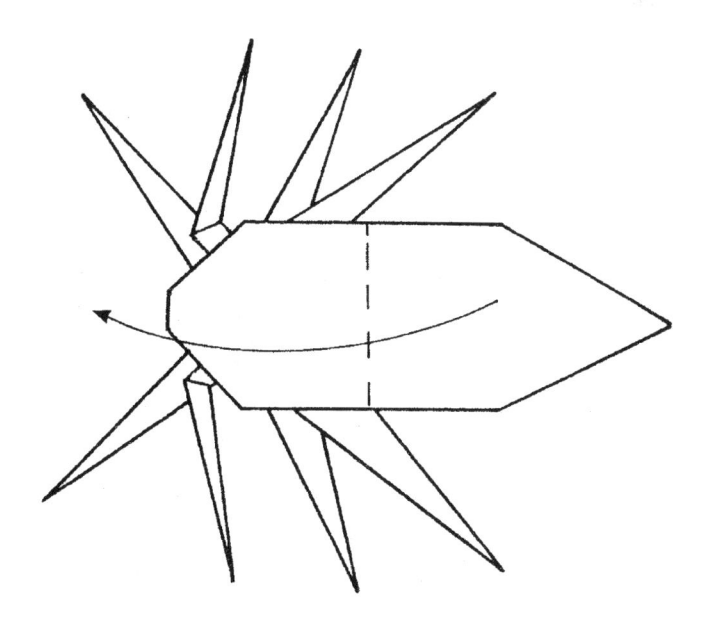

Step 6

(Upper image) Fold nose behind and seal tightly with a small piece of tape. Now crease-fold the model in half and round out its body. Fold the tiny feet in directions shown and then turn the model over.

(Lower image) Shown upside down, make sure the tape holds the nose back. As mentioned previously, the nose point could be cut into two and folded forward to make two small pincers.

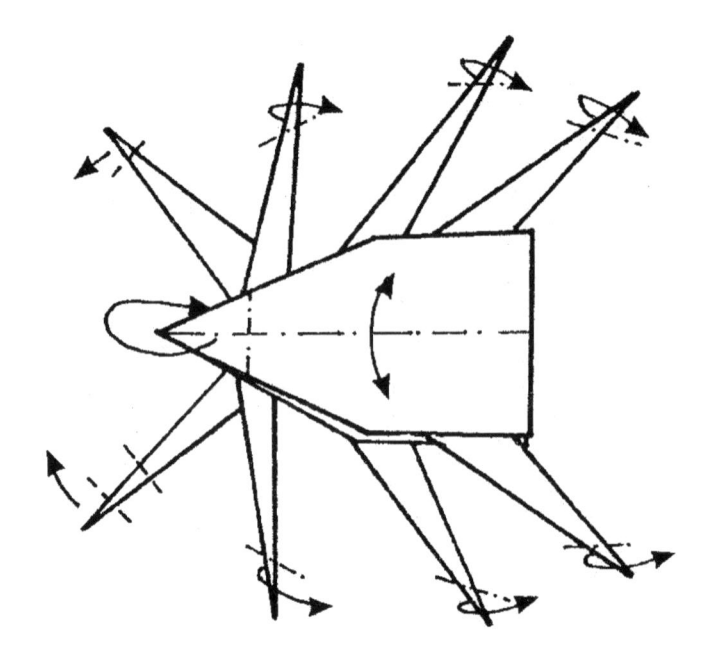

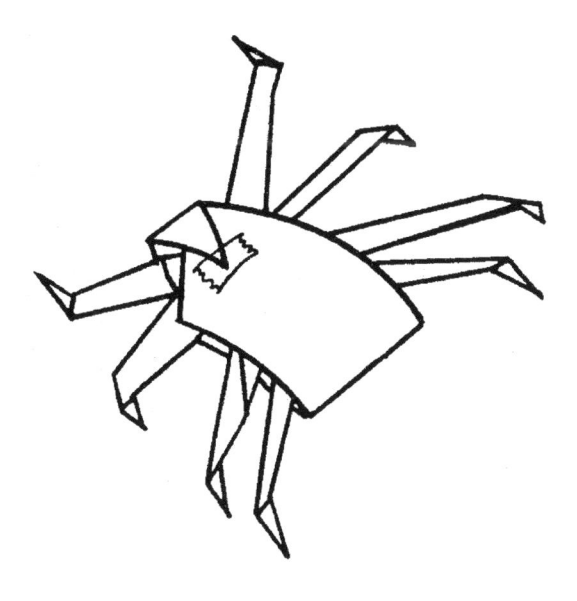

Step 7

Your completed spider is now ready to scare the wits out of someone. Fold a few black ones for Halloween.

Grasshopper

Considered by some to bring good luck, these jumping critters have played havoc with our crops throughout history. Species such as locusts destroy huge areas of vegetation in a single swarm.

Grasshoppers lay their eggs in the soil and can grow up to 11 centimeters long. Our grasshopper will be a little more passive.

Step 1

Begin with the Bird Base facing you width wise, the two points pointing left. Outside reverse fold these points. Flip the bottom right-hand flap to the left.

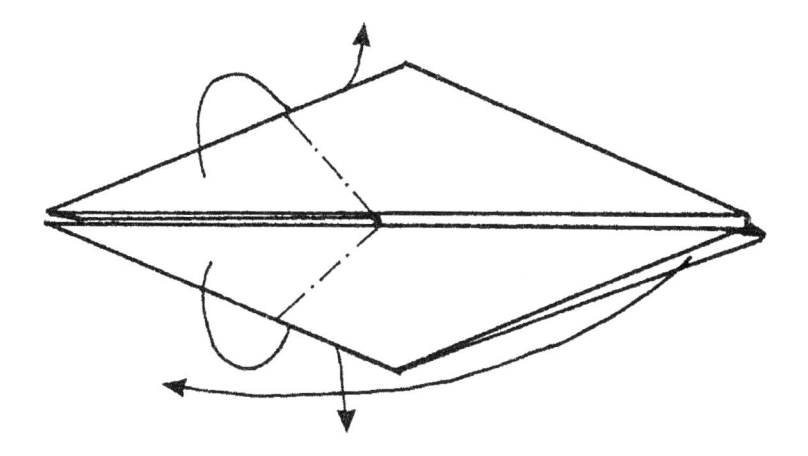

Step 2

Fold upper triangle section from right to left.

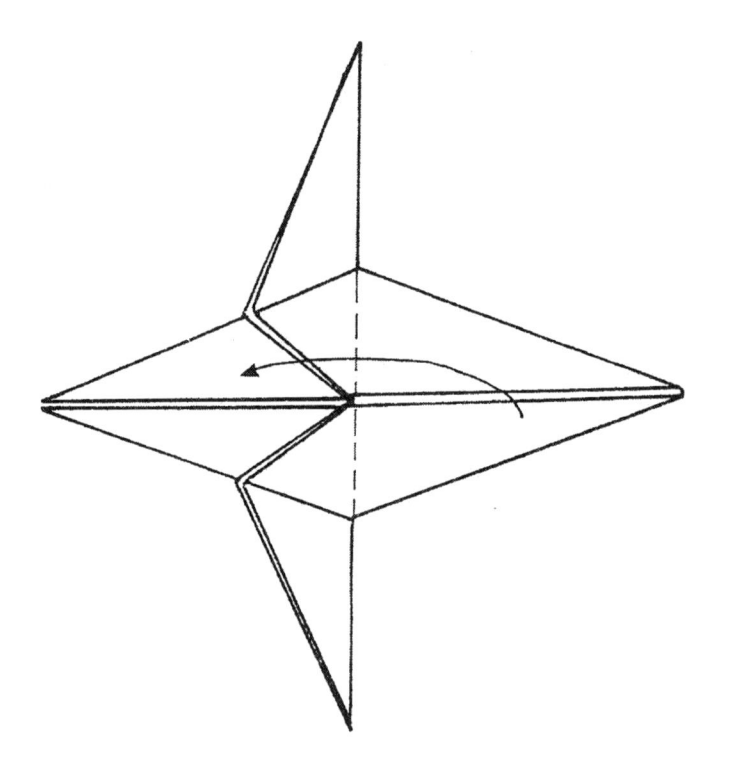

Step 3

Fold point A to meet point B as for the Dragonfly wing, however, the crease will fold all the way to the point X.

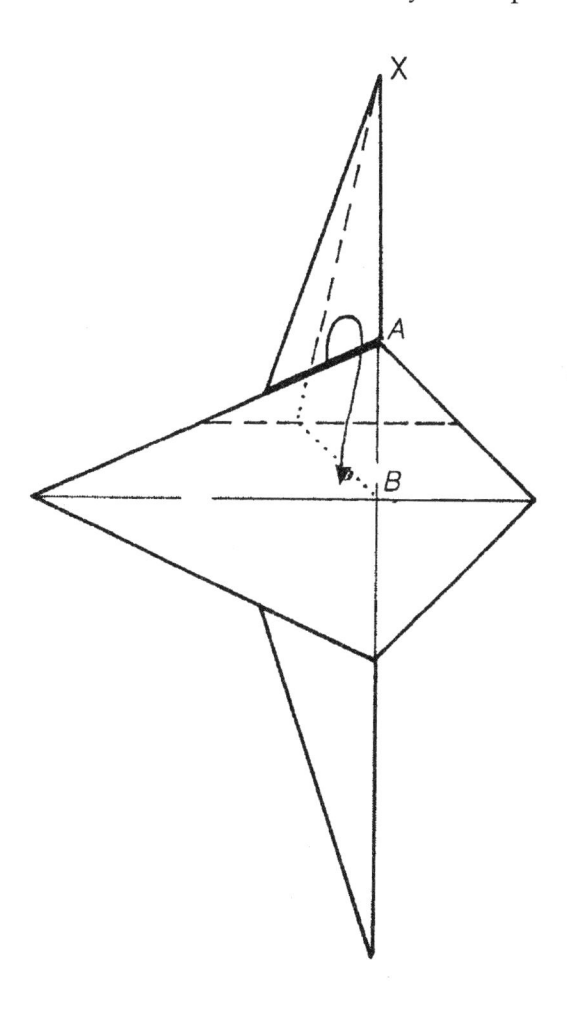

Step 4

Almost there; flatten and repeat for the other side.

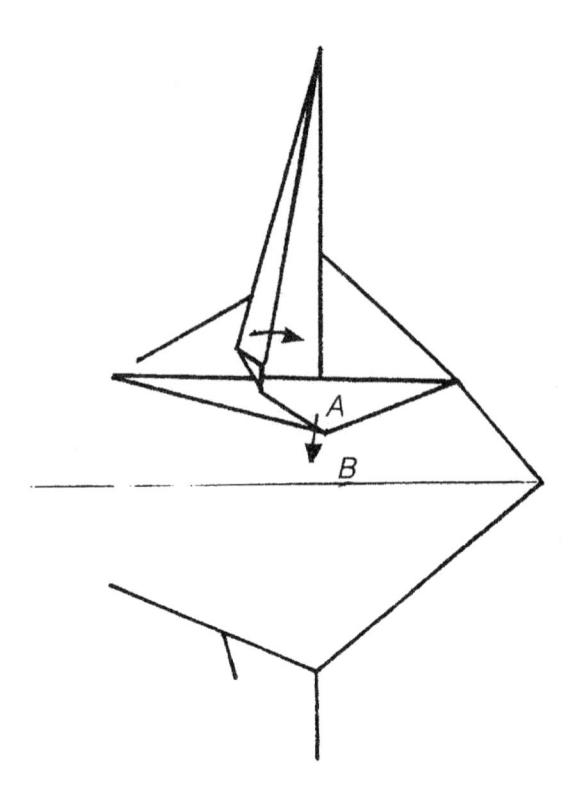

Step 5

Snip right through the middle of the legs to make three legs on either side.

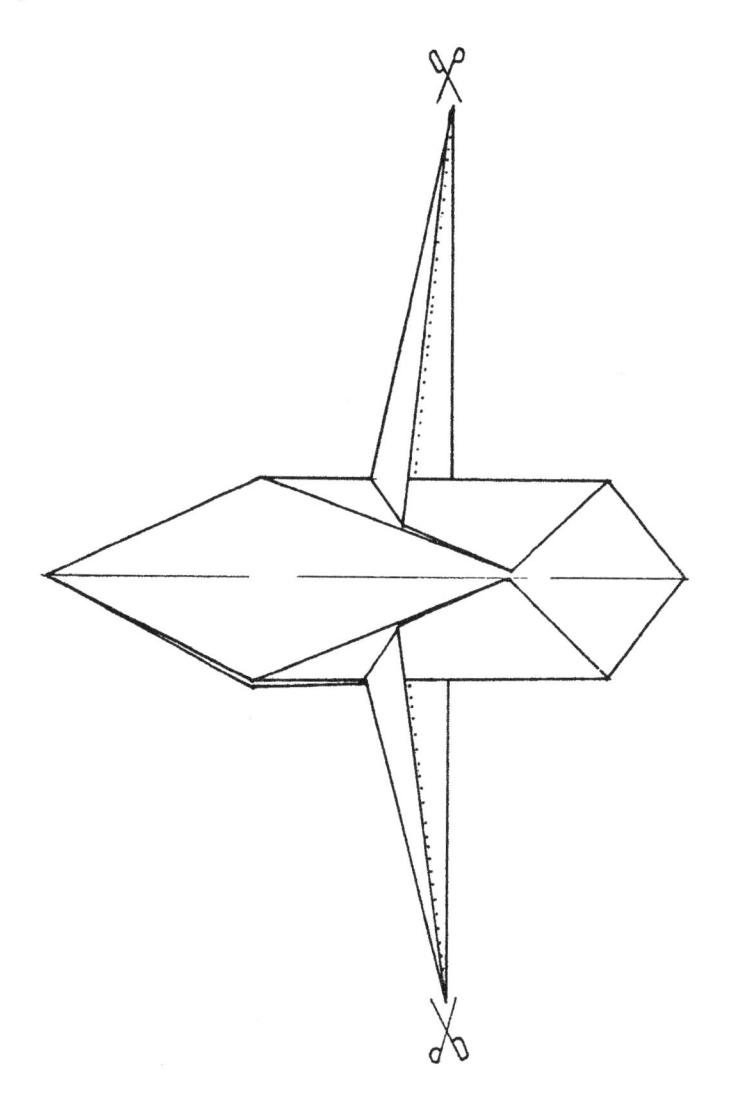

Step 6

(Left image) Leg section; reverse fold the outer leg to the left.

(Right image) Make a crease-fold on the center-right leg along XX. Note fold halfway down this leg too. Make an inverse fold for the lower leg Y to the right, positioning it behind the center leg.

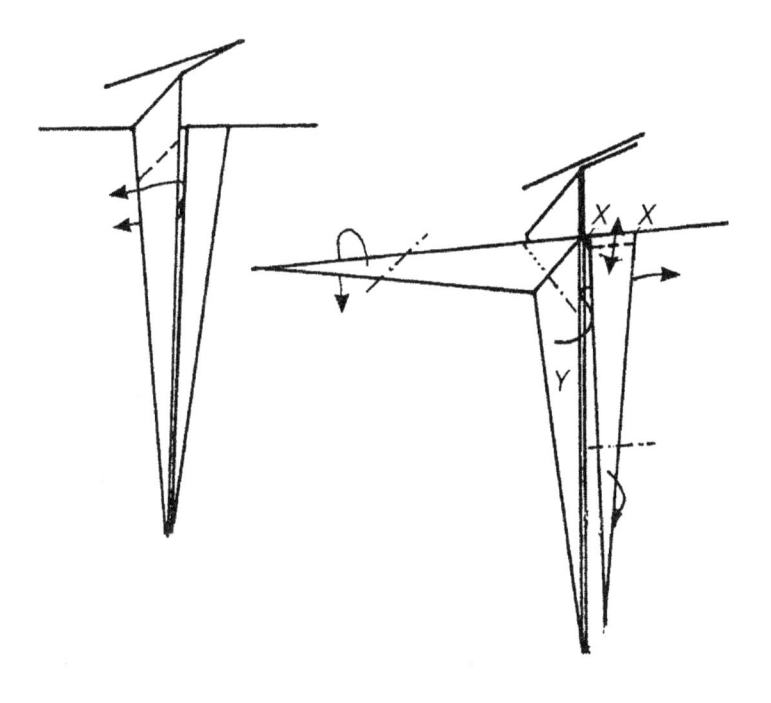

Step 7

Fold end of leg Y behind where shown. Now repeat preceding steps for the other side.

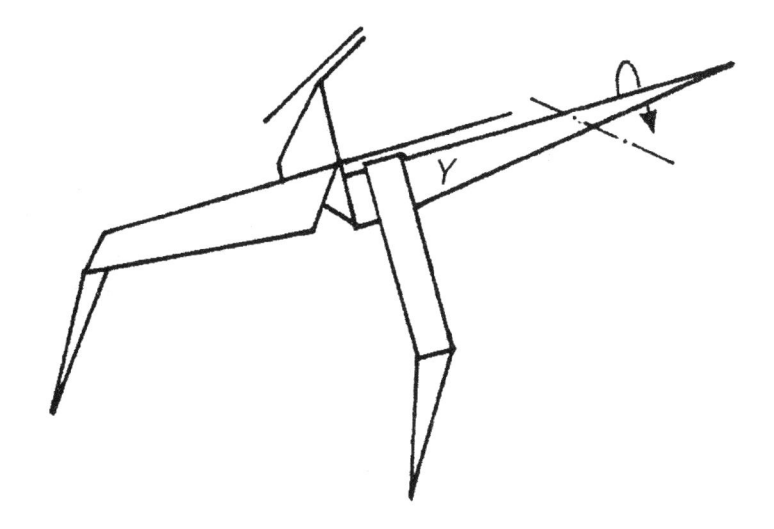

Step 8

Your critter is taking shape nicely. Snip through the top layer to form the wings. Fold these wings across to the right.

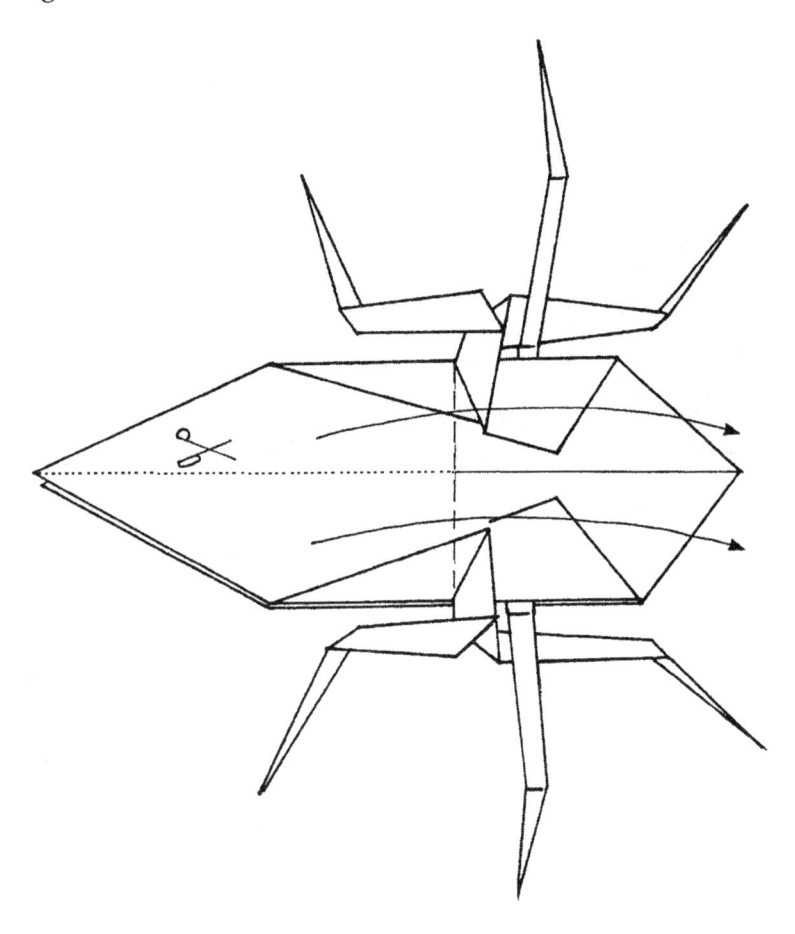

Step 9

Fold entire model in half along the length of the body.

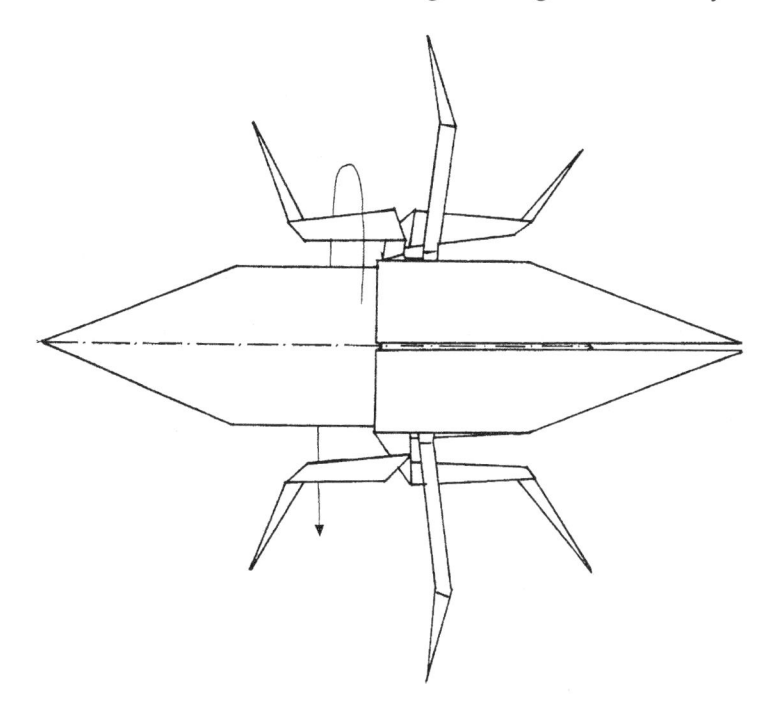

Step 10

Reverse fold the head section. Fold up the leg section so that it is at right angles to the body on each side.

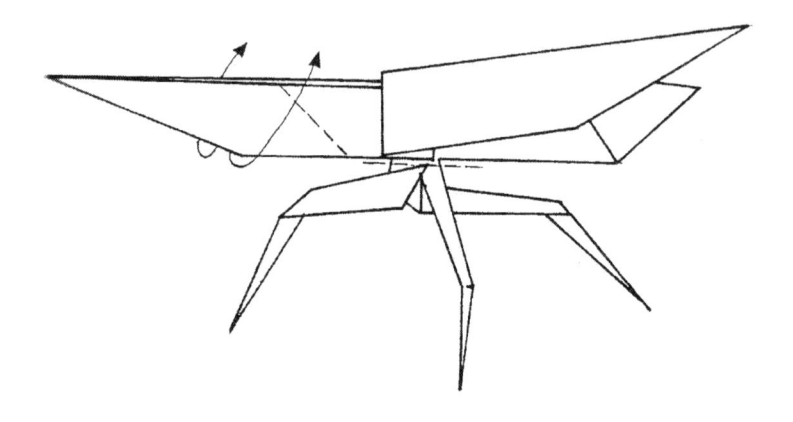

Step 11

For the head, reverse fold the point downwards and then fold right-hand edges to left, pushing in the corner. Finally, inverse fold the point, tucking it inside the head.

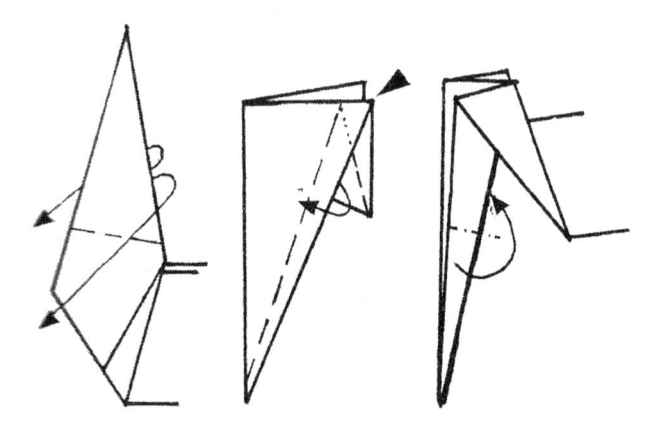

Step 12

Your completed Grasshopper is shown below. Tie a string to a little green one and confuse the cat. Or make a few for good luck. Or make a hundred for your own swarm. Just hop to it!

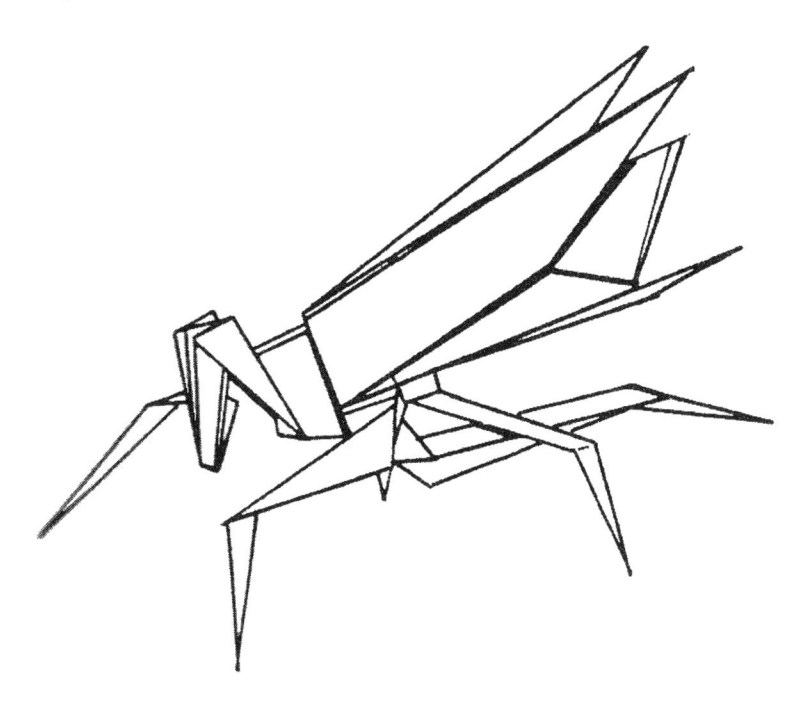

Made in the USA
San Bernardino, CA
07 July 2019